A DARK HISTORY:
THE BIBLE

A DARK HISTORY:
THE BIBLE

THE SINS, THE TEMPTATION,
THE BETRAYAL, AND THE WORD

MICHAEL KERRIGAN

METRO BOOKS
New York

METRO BOOKS
New York

An Imprint of Sterling Publishing
1166 Avenue of the Americas
New York, NY 10036

Editorial and design by
Amber Books Ltd
74–77 White Lion Street
London N1 9PF
www.amberbooks.co.uk

Project Editor: Sarah Uttridge
Designer: Jerry Williams
Picture Research: Terry Forshaw

ISBN: 978-1-4351-5943-3

For information about custom editions, special sales, and premium and corporate purchases,
please contact Sterling Special Sales at 800-805-5489 or specialsales@sterlingpublishing.com.

Manufactured in China

2 4 6 8 10 9 7 5 3 1

www.sterlingpublishing.com

CONTENTS

Incipit prologus sancti iheronimi
presbiteri i parabolas salomonis
ungat epistola quos iungit sacerdoti
um: immo carta non diuidat: quos
xpi nectit amor. Comentarios in osee.
amos ⁊ zachariam malachiam quoq;
poscitis. Scripsisse: si licuisset preuali
tudine. Mittitis solacia sumptuum.
notarios nostros et librarios sustenta
ns: ut vobis potissimum nostrum desudet
ingenium. Et ecce ex latere frequens turba
diuersa poscentium: quasi aut equum sit me
vobis esurientibus aliis laborare: aut
in ratione dati et accepti cuiusque preter
vos obnoxius sim. Itaq; longa egrota
tione fractus: ne penitus hoc anno re
ticere. ⁊ apud vos mutus essem: viduum
opus nomini vestro consecraui: interp
tatione videlicet trium salomonis vo
luminum: masloth qd hebrei pabolas.
vulgata editio puerbia vocat: coeleth
que grece ecclesiasten. latine acionatore
possumus dicere: sirasirim qd i linguam
nostram vertit canticu canticorum. Fertur et
panaretos. iesu filii sirach liber: ⁊ alius
pseudographus. qui sapientia salo
monis inscribitur. Quorum priore hebra
icum reperi. non ecclesiasticu ut apud la
tinos: sed pabolas prenotatum. Cui iuncti
erant ecclesiastes. et canticu canticorum: ut
similitudine salomonis. non solum nu
mero librorum: sed etiam materiax gene
re coequaret. Secundus apud hebreos
nusquam est: quia et ipse stilus grecam
eloquentiam redolet: et nonnulli scriptor
veteres hunc esse iudei filonis affirmant.
Sicut ergo iudith ⁊ thobie ⁊ macha
beorum libros. legit quidem eos ecclesia. sed
inter canonicas scripturas non recipit:
sic ⁊ hec duo volumina legat ad edi
ficatione plebis: non ad auctoritatem
ecclesiasticorum dogmatum affirmandam.

Si cui sane septuaginta interpretum
magis editio placet: habet eam a nobis
olim emendatam. Neq; enim noua sic cu
dimus: ut vetera destruamus. Et tamen cu
diligentissime legerit: sciat magis nostra
scripta intelligi: que non in tertium vas
transfusa coacuerit: sed statim de prelo
purissime ⁊ emendata teste: suum saporem ser
uauerit. Incipiunt parabole salomonis

Arabole salomonis
filii dauid regis isrl:
ad sciendam sapienti
am ⁊ disciplinam: ad
intelligenda verba
prudentie et suscipi
endam eruditatione doctrine: iusticiam
et iudicium ⁊ equitatem: ut detur paruulis
astutia: et adolescenti scientia et intel
lectus. Audies sapiens sapientior erit: ⁊
intelliget gubernacla possidebit. Ani
aduertet parabolam et interpretatio
nem: verba sapientum ⁊ enigmata eorum.
Timor domini principium sapientie. Sapien
tiam atq; doctrinam stulti despiciunt.
Audi fili mi disciplinam patris tui et ne
dimittas legem matris tue: ut addatur
gracia capiti tuo: ⁊ torques collo tuo.
Fili mi si te lactauerint peccatores: ne ac
quiescas eis. Si dixerint veni nobiscu
insidiemur sanguini: abscondamus te
diculas contra insontem frustra. degluti a
mus eum sicut infernus viuentem ⁊ inte
grum: quasi descendentem in lacum: omine
preciosam substantiam reperiemus: implebimus
domus nostras spoliis. sortem mitte no
biscum. marsupium sit unum omnium
nostrum: fili mi ne ambules cum eis. Pro
hibe pedem tuum a semitis eorum. Pedes
enim illorum ad malum currunt: ⁊ festinant ut
effundant sanguinem. Frustra autem
iacitur rete ante oculos pennatorum. Ipsi q;
contra sanguinem suum insidiantur: et

INTRODUCTION

Murder, treachery, rape and war: anyone who looks to the Bible for either spiritual reassurance or moral guidance may end up with much more than they bargained for.

◆

'The darkness and the light are both alike to thee.' PSALM 139.

B ad things happen in the 'Good Book'. Not surprisingly, perhaps: its 'goodness' has to a considerable extent been thrust upon it in modern retrospect; it's actually the product of a distant – and a very different – time. The idea that we should turn its pages for spiritual comfort and moral edification is comparatively new – and makes demands on the Bible that it struggles to fulfil. This is not to say that such sustenance isn't to be found in the Bible's pages – of course it is. Just that

Opposite: Produced in the 1450s, the 'Gutenberg Bible' was the first book to be printed using movable type. Old as it is, the Bible has never been far from the forefront of Western history's political tumults and of its spiritual and cultural revolutions.

it takes a reader who is predisposed to be receptive – and at times a bit selective.

These limitations may be structural: once we accept the Bible's premise that the whole of humanity is descended from a single couple, then we have to acknowledge its easy acceptance of incest among our remoter forebears. (A certain capacity for denial is needed – even for 'fundamentalists', few of whom can really find the time and energy to become seriously exercised about the evils of mixing wool and linen – Leviticus 19, 19). Other shortcomings (if that's really what they are, as these are matters of perspective) simply show the vastness of the cultural and social changes that have taken place in the thousands of years since the earliest Israelites (a small, largely pastoralist people) walked the earth. The 'realities' of life – even the apparently 'timeless' ones – have been transformed by everything from democratic politics to the germ theory of disease; from air travel to anaesthesia and women's rights.

A Decent Decalogue

The Ten Commandments are all very well: murder, most of us would agree, is wrong, covetousness is a corrosive feeling and adultery undermines the happiness of whole families. But the Commandments' emphasis on the need to avoid idolatry, understandable as this is in its biblical context, has seemed strange for centuries – certainly for the whole of the Christian period. (Hence the rage to rationalize

Below: 'And he went unto his father's house at Ophrah, and slew his brethren … being threescore and ten persons, upon one stone' (9, 5). The Book of Judges reports the crimes of Abimelech (depicted here by Gustav Doré) almost gleefully.

'THE THING WHICH HE DID'

PERSPECTIVE IS ALL, and every generation re-creates the Bible in its own image. However firm we think we are in our belief, we're invariably selective in what we see. While modern readers have successfully turned a blind eye to scripturally-sanctioned incest, polygamy and genocide, they've also tended to see sins that just aren't there. Take the notorious case of Onan: that unfortunate son of Judah has been forever identified with the 'sin' of masturbation.

That the Bible, while certainly condemning Onan, makes no such judgement against him is clear to anyone who reads his story (Genesis 38, 8):

And Judah said unto Onan, Go in unto thy brother's wife, and marry her, and raise up seed to thy brother. And Onan knew that the seed should not be his; and it came to pass, when he went in unto his brother's wife, that he spilled it on the ground, lest that he should give seed to his brother. And the thing which he did displeased the Lord.

What it was that 'displeased the Lord', it seems, had little or nothing to do with the 'sin' of 'onanism'. (Onan's crime may even have been one of *coitus interruptus*, some scholars say.) It certainly doesn't seem to have been the act of masturbation *per se* that offended God but his deliberate and defiant withholding of his semen; his refusal to serve his sister-in-law as his father had directed.

> 'As authoritative as it seems, as sonorously as it's written, the "Word" of God is open to unnumerable interpretations'.

these decrees as injunctions against the 'worship' of worldly things like sex or money.) And, if it's wrong to kill, what of all that smiting? From the Book of Joshua onwards, the Bible is full of it. What of Samson (Judges 16, 28)? Should we see his death as justifying the suicide bombers of our own age?

Abimelech's slaughter of the 70 princes who apparently impede his path to the throne occasions no particular editorial comment in Judges 9. David's affair with Bathsheba, and his murderous plot against her husband Uriah (2 Samuel 11), are condemned and divinely punished, although the king is held up as an example for all generations thereafter.

And what of the Bible's more implicit rulings – those it doesn't assert outright yet appears to exemplify: its disapproval of Miriam's defiance of her brother Moses (Numbers 12, 1), for example? There's no doubt that Miriam's waywardness offends the Lord (she's afflicted with leprosy in punishment), but is it as God's appointed leader, or simply as a man, a brother – a male – that Moses should have been revered?

Open to Interpretation

As authoritative as it seems, as sonorously as it's written, the 'Word' of God is open to innumerable interpretations. This really shouldn't come as a great surprise, of course. Any text is, pretty much by definition,

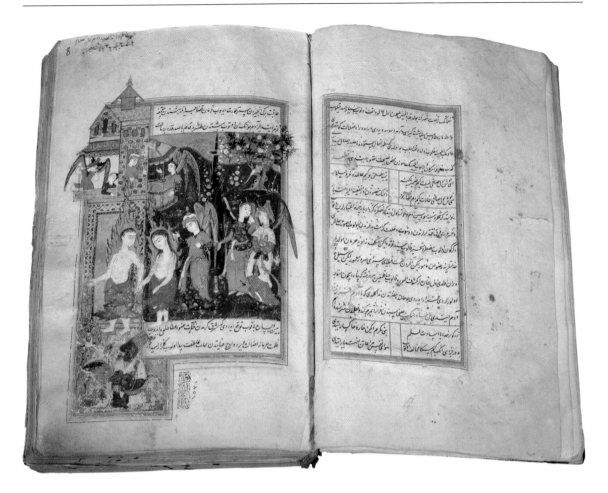

susceptible to a range of different readings. When that 'text' is actually, like the Bible, a collection of several different texts, the possibilities are multiplied many times. To the 24 books of the *Tanakh* – the Hebrew Bible – Christian Bibles add certain 'deuterocanonical books', and, of course, an entire 'New Testament' devoted to the life and teachings of Christ and his disciples. Well over 50 different books, then, each with its own doctrinal angle, spiritual emphasis and composition history: the Bible is an enormously complex text. Even this

understates the problem, though: many of these texts overlap in narrative content and subject matter. In the New Testament, for instance, the gospels of Matthew, Mark, Luke and John all deal with substantially the same events. These are relatively easy to unravel, though. The prophetic books that form the poetic heart of the Old Testament are impossible to order, loose as they are in their narrative formation and oblique as they are in their approach – in many cases to the same few events, such as the sacking of Jerusalem or the Babylonian Captivity.

Right: The prestige possessed by the Bible was inevitably coveted by wealthy rulers: the 'Urbinate Bible' was commissioned by the Duke of Urbino, Italy, in the 1470s. Here, at the start of Exodus, Moses leads the Jews out of their captivity.

filiox ifrl qui ingrefli sunt in ægyptū cùm Iacob
singuli cū domib, suis introierūt Ruben: Syme
on: Leui: Iudas: ysachar: zabulon et Beniamin
Dan: et Neptalim. Gad: et Afer: Erant igitur
omnæ animæ eoxq egrefli sūt de femore Iacob
septuagita. Iofeph autē in ægypto erat. Quo
mortuo et uniuerfis frib, eius: omnū q, cognatio
ne sua. filii ifrl creuerūt et quasi germinantes
multiplicati sū. ac roborati nimis impleuerūt
terrā. Surrexit interea rex nouus super ægyptū
qui ignorabat Iofeph. Et ait ad pplm suum. Ec
ce populus filiox ifrael mltus et fortior nobis es
Venite sapienter opprimamus eū: ne forte mul
tiplicetur: et si ingruerit contra nos bellū: ad
datur nris inimicis: expugnatis q, nobis egredi
atur de terra. Prepofuit itaq, magistros operū
ut affligerēt eos oneribz: ædificauerūt q, urbes
tabernaculox Pharaoni Phiton: et Ramefses
quātoq, opprimebant eos: tanto magis multi
plicabantur: et crescebat. Oderant q, filios ifrl
ægyptii: et affligebāt illudentes eis: atq, ad a
maritudinē perducebant uitā eox operibus
duris luti: et laterix: omni q, famulatu quo in
terræ opibus premebātur. Dixit autē rex ę
gypti obstetricibus hebreox: quax una uoca
batur Sephora: altera Phua: precipiēs eis. Qn

obstetricabitis hebreas: et partus tēpus aduene
rit: si masculus fuerit interficite eū: si femina
reseruate. Timuerunt obstetrices deum: et nō
fecerunt iuxta preceptū regis ægypti: sed con
seruabāt mares. Quibz ad se accersitis rex ait
Quid nā est hoc quod facere uoluistis ut puēos
seruaretis: Quæ rnderūt. Non sūt hebreæ si
cut ægyptiæ mulieres. Ipæ enim obstetricādi
hēnt scientiā: et priusq, ueniamus ad eas pa
rūt. Bene ergo fecit deus obstetricibz. Et cre
uit pplus cōfortatus q, est nimis. Et qa timue
rūt obstetrices deū: ædificauit illis domos. Pre
cepit autē Pharao omni pplo suo dicēs. Quicqd
masculini sexus natū fuerit: in flumē proicite
quicqd feminī reseruate. · C II ·
Greffus est post hæc uir de domo leui accepta
uxore stirpis suæ: q cōcepit et peperit filium.
Et uidēs eum elegantē: abscōdit mensibz tribz.
cūq, iam celare non poffet: sumpsit fiscelam
scirpeā: et liniuit eā bitumie ac pice: posu
it q, intus infantulū: et exposuit eū in carep
to fluminis stāte procul sorore eius: et cōsi
derāte euentū rei. Ecce autē descēdebat fi
lia Pharaonis ut lauaretur in flumine: et pu
ellæ eius gradiebātur p crepidinē aluei. Quæ
cū uidiffet fiscellā in papirione: misit unā de

Nor do the difficulties end there: although vaguely seen as representing the 'Word of God', the books of the Bible are the work of human authors – and mostly multiple human authors at that. The tradition that Moses wrote the Torah or, as it's been known to Christians, as the 'Pentateuch' (because it comprises the first five books of the Bible: Genesis, Exodus, Leviticus, Numbers and Deuteronomy) hasn't been taken seriously by scholars for a long, long time. Rather, the tendency has been for these works to have been brought together from a number of different, pre-existing sources – which may well themselves have been written by a number of different scribes working some time around the sixth century BCE.

Likewise, the later books of the Old Testament, including those that announce with seeming authority that they're the Books of Isaiah, Daniel, Jeremiah and so forth. (There may indeed, it's believed, be bits of writing by a man named Jeremiah in the book that bears his name, but they're just snatches of a finished work that represents a stew of different sources.) The haphazardness of the Bible's construction is marked not only by the notorious double-creation of man and woman, but by some of the more mind-boggling moments in the Book of Proverbs. 'Answer not a fool according to his

Above: Clutching his brow in disgust at the decadence he sees, the Prophet Jeremiah seems real in this illustration from the *National Illustrated Family Bible* (c. 1870). But it's hard to know how much of 'his' book he wrote – even if he actually existed.

folly,' it counsels (26, 4), 'lest thou also be like unto him.' 'Answer a fool according to his folly,'

'THE BOOKS'

THE BIBLE SEEMS to have taken its name from the Phoenician port of Biblos, in what is now northern Lebanon. 'Paper' made from papyrus reeds was shipped there from Egypt, so the legend went. The explanation would have been more convincing if the Bible had actually been written on papyrus-paper – mostly, it seems,

parchment was used. In its way, though, the survival of the story is the perfect illustration of the power of myth: justified or not, the word *biblia* became used for 'books', and so it stuck. As a title for the scripture, the word seems at first to have been used only in the Christian tradition. Only later was it taken up by Jews.

it recommends in the very next verse, 'lest he be wise in his own conceit.'

Chronicle or Code?

To add still more to the confusion, there are the questions of what the purpose of the Bible was (when it was written); what its function *has been* (as read and interpreted in the centuries since); and what it *is* as we approach it, from our own individual standpoint, in the present day.

If it's difficult to establish what the Bible actually 'says' on a given question, that's in part because it is impossible for us to be absolutely clear on what the terms of reference are.

To what extent, for instance, was it ever intended to offer guidance? To *some* extent, certainly. As we've seen, great swathes of Exodus and Leviticus are devoted to the codification of Jewish law. Christians (and modern Jews) must interpret (or dispense with) these scriptural strictures as they see fit. But at the same time, and in many ways more obviously, the Bible, far from being a catalogue of rules, was written as a chronicle of a people's history. This distinction brings caveats all of its own: no ancient chronicler felt himself bound by the conventions of factual truth that govern even tabloid journalism, let alone academic historiography. But it also raises questions of how exemplary the events of the Bible are supposed to be.

Above: 'The waters which came down from above stood and rose up upon an heap …' allowing Joshua and the Jews to walk dry-shod across the River Jordan (Joshua 3, 16). A literal claim or a poetic flight?

No one would suggest that, because General Patton and his U.S. Third Army crossed the Rhine on such-and-such a day in 1945, this should modify our actions in any area of our lives. Yet this example illustrates how different the Bible is from any other history. Large as it has loomed in the consciousness of the last

Above: India's *Rig Veda* is believed by scholars to be significantly older than the Bible. But it offers intriguing parallels with the Middle Eastern work – in its account of the world's first origins, for example.

whole. Since that tradition has provided the intellectual and cultural underpinning for progress in those western countries (in Europe and North America) that have led the world in power and affluence in recent centuries, that's meant a highly privileged status for the Bible – even among the religiously apathetic.

The *Rig Veda*, written down around 500 BCE, although almost certainly passed down through oral recitation for at least 1000 years before that, is held in high regard in Indian culture, but relegated to the realm of 'myth' elsewhere. Hymn CXXIX describes the moment before creation in terms that are completely familiar to readers of the Bible :

Darkness there was: at first concealed in darkness this All was undiscriminated chaos. All that existed then was void and formless.

So too for the Norse *Völuspá*:
Sea nor cool waves nor sand there were; Earth had not been, nor heaven above, But a yawning gap, and grass nowhere.

It is interesting that, for the seafaring Norsemen, the idea of the primeval void was not to be suggested by the image of an ocean: rather, it was the absence of waves and seacoasts that made the 'gap' so unimaginable.

It's no particular surprise to find a Middle-Eastern people like the Jews sharing assumptions about the creation with the Hittites, Sumerians and other Mesopotamian cultures. In these traditions too, everything emerges out of a primeval chaos, which is then shaped into a world by divine force. Hesiod, Greek poet of the seventh century BCE, shared this view (very likely because he was directly influenced by it). Great myths think alike, then, regarding creation and a great many other things. The difference is that the Bible – even when we don't actually

decades, the Second World War was never paradigmatic for us in quite the same way that – say – the Conquest of Canaan by the Israelites was long supposed to be.

From Myth to Mainstream

In so far as it is a chronicle, the Bible also has the status of an 'origin myth': first for the Jews, then for the 'Judeo-Christian tradition' as a

EXEGETICAL ENERGY

ANY TEXT, WE'VE seen, is open to differences of interpretation. The longer and denser it is, the richer the readings that can be found. A text like this seems to transcend itself: there's so much more there than 'the words on the page' – and then the commentary it generates can open up a whole new dimension.

The Bible is both the original and the ultimate text of this kind for the Western tradition: big and complex as it is, it busts out of its covers as we read. From early on, the challenges it offered scholars – in its obscurities, its contradictions, its seeming lacunas – gave rise to an industry of exegesis (explanatory criticism) and commentary. The *midrashim* of early Jewish tradition didn't just attempt to iron out the difficulties: often they tried to make good the gaps, adding narratives and characters of their own. The story of Lilith is one example.

Paradoxically, it seems a bigger book for being able to be read in tiny sections, such as the daily readings of the pious

Christian, for example. But it's also lent itself historically to the sort of divinatory reading a pagan priest might have made of animal entrails or a flight of birds (or a modern medium reading tea leaves): often people have opened it at random to find guidance in their daily lives.

Right: St Jerome translating the Bible into Latin: centuries after the Fall of Rome, Jerome's new 'Vulgate' version opened up this complex text for interpretation, reinterpretation, discussion and debate.

believe it – seems somehow to have transcended the world of myth.

Tricks and Tradition

That conceded, studying the Bible in the context of other mythic traditions can help elucidate much that might otherwise seem obscure. For one thing, the outrageous amorality it shows – with apparent approval

– on occasion: the deceptions by which Jacob cheated his brother Esau out of his birthright and his father's blessing. These stories may not be particularly edifying, but they tally perfectly with examples from other comparable traditions of what anthropologists have called the 'trickster myth'. From Odysseus, deviser of the Trojan Horse, to Brer Rabbit in the American folktale, ingenious frauds have proven perversely popular. They offer life-lessons, if not necessarily ethical instruction.

The other thing about myths is that they tell a people who they are, embodying what would otherwise just be a 'background'. Stories like this lend life and colour to what would

> 'What makes the Bible so bewildering, so impossible to encompass, is what makes it so enriching for readers'.

otherwise be a pallid, genealogical inheritance; they help to construct a cultural identity that really seems worth identifying with.

Not that background in the more abstract sense isn't significant in itself: hence the Bible's notorious 'begats'. From Genesis 5, 9, for example:

And Enos lived ninety years, and begat Cainan; … And Cainan lived seventy years, and begat Mahalaleel … And Mahalaleel lived sixty and five years and begat Jared … And Jared lived an hundred sixty and two years, and he begat Enoch … And Enoch lived sixty and five years, and begat Methuselah…

Left: Methusaleh occupies a twelfth-century stained-glass window in Canterbury Cathedral. Just as Genesis' genealogies established a sense of lineage for the Jews, the Bible as a whole gave Western Christians a sense of spiritual inheritance.

That Methuselah went on to live for 'nine hundred sixty and nine years' (5, 27) suggests that these lifespans too are what we would describe as mythical. It's striking too how pointless this sort of cataloguing seems from a modern historical perspective: no attempt whatsoever is made to describe the specific contribution made by any of these patriarchs or the society over which they were to preside. At the same time, though, these listings can be seen to recall the Sumerian King List or the pharaonic chronology to be found on the Palermo Stone. For the Jews, as for the Sumerians and Egyptians, it was more important to establish legitimacy through a clear continuity of generations than to offer information on what the world was like at any given time.

The Book of Life – and Death

Ultimately, what makes the Bible so bewildering, so impossible to encompass, is what makes it so enriching for readers of every kind. That goes for its ethical challenges as well as its textual cruces. In finding space for rape and genocide it's like life, in other words; Sarah's jealousy would strike a chord with any wife. Sure, we can, if we're determined to, hover fastidiously over the Bible's text to extract a few uplifting anecdotes for our edification. It's hard to see in that case how we'd really be engaging with a work whose 'darkness' is what makes it truly human. Or, for that matter, with any of the real challenges of life. The point about the Bible is that it contains the whole of existence, from alpha to omega, from creation to apocalypse: it may not be in every sense a 'good book', but it is a great one.

GENESIS: FALL, FRATRICIDE AND FLOOD

'Let there be light,' came the famous fiat, but hardly was God's creation complete than human disobedience plunged everything back into darkness and sin.

'Darkness was upon the face of the deep.' GENESIS 1, 2.

First things first. 'In the beginning', the Book of Genesis tells us, 'God created the heaven and the earth.' The idea of higher and lower states is central from the start. The difference is all-important: this is to be a universe articulated in the first instance by its divisions and its distinctions ('And God divided the light from the darkness', 1, 4), and only secondarily by its definitions of what things

Opposite: Everything began with God (above). But, as the alpha and omega of his holy book remind us (left), he defines our end as well. Here an angel exhibits the treasures of the earth, holding up an astrolabe (an antique model of the heavens).

are ('And God called the light Day, and the darkness he called Night', 1, 5).

Order is to be important too. No time is lost in establishing the essential rhythms and routines of earthly existence ('And the evening and the morning were the first day', 1, 5).

'And God saw that it was good,' we're told (1, 13), and yet what has clearly been a codification, a laying-down of laws, inevitably brings with it at least an implicit thought of rule-breaking, of disorder. The goodness of God's creation has been summed up in his command that there should be 'light' (1, 3); but every day, we've already been told, contains its darkness – 'night'.

Man and Woman

The stars; the sun and moon; 'the moving creature that hath life, and fowl that may

Above: Man, said his creator, was made 'in our image, after our likeness'. The Renaissance liked to take him at his word. Michelangelo's famous scene from the Sistine Chapel (c. 1511) makes the very most of the majestic beauty of the human form.

fly above the earth'; the 'great whales', 'fish' and 'cattle' and the 'creeping thing'. Having brought all these beasts into being, God decides (1, 26) to 'make man in our image, after our likeness', resolved to give him 'dominion over the fish of the sea, and over the fowl of the air, and over the cattle'. That man is made 'in the image of God' only underlines his special status among the wonders of creation: 'Behold', says God:

I have given you every herb bearing seed, which is upon the face of all the earth, and every tree, in the which is the fruit of a tree yielding seed; to you it shall be for meat.

So Good He Made them Twice

'So God created man in his own image,' says the Book of Genesis (1, 27): 'in the image of God he created him'. Does the male pronoun encompass the female too? It seems to – at least to begin with, verse 27 continuing immediately on to elaborate: 'male and female created he them'.

That appears to be the end of it. God's creation is complete, the whole thing being rounded off with the now customary note that God saw that it was 'good'. Just a few lines later, though, in Chapter 2, verse 7, we find ourselves starting over: 'the Lord God formed man of the dust of the ground, and breathed into his nostrils the breath of life, and man became a living soul.'

And still no sign of Eve. Adam is alone when (2, 8) he's given his own 'Garden eastward in Eden' as a home. Only afterwards does God consider that 'It is not good that the man should be alone' and resolves to make 'an help meet' for him. Even then, there's the business of 'every

Right: Winds blow; the sun and moon both shine; fish, fowl, cattle and other creatures throng around as God completes his labours with the 'birth' of woman (2, 21). Eve emerges fully-formed from the side of her (miraculously sleeping) husband.

GOLDEN AGE

THE IDEA THAT the first men and women lived untroubled lives in a land of endless ease and pleasure was by no means unusual among ancient cultures. For the Greek poet Hesiod, in the seventh century BCE, he said that our first forebears were lucky enough to live during a 'Golden Age':

They lived like gods and felt no sorrow. They did not toil, nor did they grow old, but remained strong in hand and foot. They ate and drank freely, with no sufferings to dampen the mood. Even when they died, they did so easily, as if simply falling asleep. All good things came to them without asking, for the fertile earth brought forth its bounty spontaneously and without limit: they could just sit back and enjoy their ease and comfort, beloved of the gods and rich in livestock.

Hindu tradition talks of the *Krita Yuga*, a First and Perfect Age in which all were equal, with no divisions of wealth or caste; no death, disease nor even ageing; nor any need to labour in a world that gave freely of its plenty. In these traditions the 'Fall' of Man is more a series of stages of decline: the Greek Golden Age is succeeded by epochs of Silver and Bronze – and a wretched present one of Iron. But the Babylonian *Epic of Gilgamesh* has pretty much the whole story as we see it in Genesis, including a mud-made man being tempted by a woman – and even a seductive snake.

beast of the field, and every fowl of the air' being brought to Adam, so that the first man could allot them all their names. Only when that day's work is done does God cause a 'deep sleep' to fall upon him, during which 'he took one of his ribs, and closed up the flesh instead thereof'. It's Adam who names this animal too: 'This is now bone of my bones, and flesh of my flesh: she shall be called Woman, because she was taken out of man,' he says.

Already, by its second chapter, then, the Genesis account is proving problematic. The inconsistency is easily enough explained. So long, that is, as the reader is willing to accept the modern scholarly consensus that this narrative represents a composite of several different early

Left: However problematic its account of her creation, the Bible is clear on the perfection of woman as counterpart and as companion to her husband, 'the bone of my bones, and flesh of my flesh' in Adam's words (2, 23).

DEVIL WOMAN

THE EARLIEST JEWISH readers don't seem to have been much troubled by the discrepancies between Genesis' two accounts of the creation of man – and, more to the point – of womankind. Only later did it start causing concern. The difficulty was easily resolved, however: seizing upon the fact that the 'female' of Chapter 1 is never named, writers came up with the idea of an earlier woman who had to be dispensed with as she proved unworthy.

Hence the story of Lilith, Adam's first wife – a monster of insubordination and sexual rapacity; the antithesis of all approved forms of femininity. It's no surprise to find her mythical antecedents extending back into Mesopotamian demonology. No surprise because her first actual mention in the Bible comes in the Book of Isaiah, thought to have been written at least in part during the Babylonian Captivity; but also because her devilish nature suggests some such origins. Lilith didn't really come into her own till post-Biblical times, in the *Balmud Bavli* (mid-First Millennium CE) and the medieval *Alphabet of Ben Sira* and other mystic writings in which she becomes the terrifying embodiment of femininity at its most seductive and its most threatening. Sexually insatiable, irresistibly appealing, she was Freud's *vagina dentata* incarnate, her irresistible body the beguiling way to hell. In one thirteenth-century account, she abandons Adam for Samael, Archangel of Death and Destruction, her affinities and her loyalties all too clear.

Modern feminist scholars haven't of course been shy of registering their unease at the importance attributed to Eve, a woman, in the 'Fall of Man'. The Lilith legend doubles down on this tradition, removing all question of 'mere' weakness or impressionability, replacing sexist condescension with a more aggressive misogyny.

Below: The prevalence of female spirits in Mesopotamian tradition gave the Lilith legend a doubly sinister status. This devil-woman didn't just stand for the frailties generally associated with womanhood, but with all the evils associated with paganism by Jewish and Christian scholars.

'But of the tree of the
knowledge of good and evil,
thou shalt not eat of it'.

GENESIS 2,17

sources – a sometimes clumsy synthesis, if truth
be told. There's no great difficulty or 'darkness'
here, then, for most of us, but for those who'd
hope to find in the Bible a literal, factual
account of the world's origins, and our own, the
implicit warning could hardly be more clear.

Eve's Temptation

'Of every tree of the garden thou mayest freely
eat,' God tells Adam (2, 17): 'But of the tree of
the knowledge of good and evil, thou shalt not
eat of it: for in the day that thou eatest thereof
thou shalt surely die.' But the serpent – 'more
subtil', according to Genesis, 'than any beast of
the field which the Lord God had made' – sets
out to persuade Eve that this fearful warning is
just bluster on the creator's part:

*Ye shall not surely die: For God doth know
that in the day ye eat thereof, then your eyes shall
be opened, and ye shall be as gods, knowing good
and evil.*

Eve, then, takes the fruit and eats it; and she
gives it to her husband and he eats it too, 'And
the eyes of them both were opened, and they
knew that they were naked; and they sewed fig
leaves together, and made themselves aprons.'
This new-found bashfulness is what betrays
them: their efforts to conceal themselves from
God arouse his ire. 'Who told thee that thou
wast naked?' he demands. Damning the serpent

Left: *Cherchez la femme* … The serpent stays in the background
here: Eve stares insouciantly off into space as an ingenuous-
and bewildered-looking Adam takes the apple in Lucas Cranach
the Elder's classic depiction of the Fall (1526).

Above: Sent out of the sunshine of the earthly paradise into a
dark, drear wilderness, Adam and Eve can now anticipate lives
of suffering and toil. Ultimately, however, this disgrace was to
open the way to a more meaningful paradise in heaven.

to crawl upon his belly and eat dust for all his
days, he curses Eve to a life of suffering and
subjection:

*I will greatly multiply thy sorrow and thy
conception; in sorrow thou shalt bring forth children;
and thy desire shall be to thy husband, and he shall
rule over thee.*

As for Adam, his crime is in the first place to
have 'hearkened unto the voice of thy wife', and
only secondarily to have eaten the forbidden
fruit. In punishment for his transgression, he's
condemned to a life of toil, trying to coax some
sort of subsistence from an uncooperative earth.

*Cursed is the ground for thy sake; in sorrow shalt
thou eat of it all the days of thy life; Thorns also and
thistles shall it bring forth to thee; and thou shalt eat*

D'après les dessins de I. Holbein.

Der Fluch.

Wohin des Menschen Fuß auch geht,
Der Tod an seiner Seite steht. —
Er gräbt, bebaut mit ihm das Land
Und führt zu Allem ihm die Hand,
Bis daß der Mensch dann müd' und matt
Sich sehnt nach seiner Ruhestatt,
Da gräbt für alle die Beschwerden
Der Tod sein Grab in kühler Erden.

Verlag von C. Uhler.

STRANGE FRUIT

THAT THE FORBIDDEN fruit of Eden was an apple is no more than a convention: there's no biblical basis at all for such a 'fact'. Like the blonde Madonnas and blue-eyed Christs of so much medieval and Renaissance art, it's a mark of the Eurocentrism of the Christian culture to which we have been heirs. According to the Quran, and to various ancient Hindu texts, the forbidden fruit was a banana; several scholars in medieval Christendom agreed. And not just because that tropical fruit seemed more likely to be at home in a paradisal garden in the Middle East: there were good iconographic reasons for the identification. Bananas hung down in bunches – drawn down in the mass, like a fallen humanity; but each individual fruit grew upwards, as though straining separately after salvation. As recently as the eighteenth century, this notion had its supporters – including no less a figure than the great Swedish naturalist Charles Linnaeus (1707–78). His adherence to the ancient theory was immortalized in the Latin name he gave the banana in his famous taxonomy of species: the *Musa paradisiaca* or 'fruit of paradise'.

the herb of the field. In the sweat of thy face shalt thou eat bread, till thou return unto the ground; for out of it wast thou taken; for dust thou art, and unto dust shalt thou return.

Carnal Knowledge?

In eating the forbidden fruit, it's clear that the 'knowledge of good and evil' the first couple acquire is what we would nowadays call 'self-consciousness'. Hence the sudden sense of embarrassment and shame at being naked – till now not just accepted but unnoticed. It doesn't take a psychoanalyst to see the symbolic

Left: Swedish naturalist Carl Linnaeus (1707–78) is regarded as the father of modern zoology. His Latin taxonomy put the ordering of species on a scientific footing. Even so, he felt the influence of scriptural traditions.

possibilities of the serpent – the phallus personified – nor to see the 'Fall' as a transition from prepubertal 'innocence' to sexual awakening.

Prior to their Fall, it seems, Adam and Eve enjoyed an infant's blissful obliviousness to their nakedness. Did they 'enjoy' the infant's 'freedom' from adult sexuality as well? While it is of course possible that the first man and woman frolicked unselfconsciously together in their innocence, there's no suggestion in the Bible that this was so – and a strong implication that they became

Left: Holbein's 'The Curse' (1547), copied in this engraving, shows Adam condemned to till the ground, with Death as his co-worker. Eve, in the background, is seen suckling her first son, whilst spinning wool upon a distaff – ancient emblem of women's work.

THE CURSE

THE IDEA THAT menstruation is 'the curse' of Eve is these days mostly aired in a spirit of grim humour, but it's been advanced entirely seriously in the past. Writers in the Jewish midrashic tradition saw the subject of Eve as one on which they could really spread themselves, venting their misogynistic feelings to their hearts' content. Already, in Genesis, we find woman condemned to suffer sexual desire for her husband (seen as a deficit, an affliction) along with subjection to him; pain in impregnation and in childbirth. But the punishment would not end there, according to the scholars: she would have to squat 'like a beast' to urinate; to grow her hair long, like Lilith – wild and unkempt – and to keep her head covered, in the style of a mourner. She would suffer pain at the loss of her virginity and the humiliation of being a cushion for her husband thereafter – lying under him in sexual congress; she should spend much of her life apart from men and be confined to her husband's home.

aware of sexual difference only in the moments after eating the forbidden fruit.

'And Adam knew Eve his wife,' we're to be told a little later (Genesis 4, 1); 'and she conceived': this is the original reference for all

> 'What has thou done? The voice of thy brother's blood crieth unto me from the ground'.
>
> GENESIS 4, 11

those arch allusions to the idea of 'knowing' someone 'in the biblical sense'. If Christianity has had a 'problem with sex', as many of its modern critics have noted, that's been largely down to its own moralists – perhaps most notably St Paul and St Augustine. It's evident even so that there's a sexual dimension to the story in Genesis, and one that even its earliest readers could hardly have ignored.

God's first explicit pronouncement on the whole question of human sexuality comes in his angry denunciation of Eve at Genesis 3, 16. It's an aspect of her accursed state that henceforth her 'desire shall be to [her] husband' (3, 16) – her sexual longings will be part of her punishment, in other words.

Our sense that such desires should be (at least) as much a source of happiness and fulfilment as of sorrow opens up an ambiguity at the very centre of the story of the 'Fall'. This is the first hint we've had that, with all the wretchedness it brought, humanity's loss of primal innocence might have its upside – an important point, as far as Christian theology has been concerned. Medieval scholars were to write of this primal offence as a *felix culpa* or 'fortunate misdeed': it was only this first fall, this loss of the earthly paradise, that allowed humankind, redeemed by Christ's subsequent sacrifice, to aspire to everlasting life with God in Heaven. Even in more widely secular terms, it may be seen that, whatever the appeal of a life of Edenic ease, it offers little scope for striving or self-betterment. Bliss it may be, but at the same time it is a bliss that has no place for creativity or enterprise – or, it might even be suggested, for any of the things that make 'post-lapsarian' life worth living.

First Blood

Without further ceremony, then, Adam and Eve were expelled from the Garden of Eden: an angel with a flaming sword barred their return. Only then (4, 1), as far as the scripture is concerned, did human history with its cycles of generation and regeneration begin in earnest: 'And Adam knew Eve his wife, and she conceived.'

A son, named Cain, resulted; after him came another boy, Abel. They grew up not just as two brothers but two important archetypes,

with much more to their mutual suspicion than sibling rivalry. 'And Abel was a keeper of sheep', says the Bible, 'but Cain was a tiller of the ground' – two entirely different economic models, in other words. Different, and incompatible, with opposing priorities in land-use and the marshalling of resources that have caused a great many clashes over the course of human history. From the raids of the nomadic Huns in Roman times all the way down to the massacre of Rwanda's pastoralist Tutsi by the agrarian Hutu in the 1990s, the collisions between these cultures have only too often been explosive.

In the case of Cain and Abel, though, the fault – from a modern perspective, at least – seems to stem less from lifestyle clash than from a difficult deity. If his punishment of their parents, although harsh, is strictly fair, God's treatment of these two young men appears positively capricious. Both brought him pious offerings – Cain from the 'fruit of the ground' he had worked so hard to cultivate, and Abel from 'the firstlings of his flock'. The Lord 'had respect unto Abel and to his offering', the Bible tells us (4, 4). But 'unto Cain and to his offering he had not respect.'

Cain, understandably, 'was very wroth' – or angry:

and it came to pass, when they were in the field, that Cain rose up against Abel his brother, and slew him.

When God came asking for Abel, Cain claimed not to know where he was – and why should he: 'Am I my brother's keeper?' But God berated him:

What hast thou done? The voice of thy brother's blood crieth unto me from the ground' (4, 11)

Left: Francesco Bacchiacca's *Eve with Cain and Abel* offers no hint of the hatred and violence to come. Does the blue of her loincloth foreshadow the gowns of Mary, the Madonna, whose child would one day redeem Eve's sin?

THE SERPENT'S SON?

THE FIRST HUMAN ever to see the light of day after a natural birth, Cain was also the first to be conventionally conceived – if we are to believe the Book of Genesis, at any rate. One midrashic tradition, though, suggests that the Serpent in the Garden of Eden didn't just tempt Eve morally but that it also sexually seduced her: it was of this diabolical coupling that Cain was the result. The appeal of this version of the story, from the scholar's point of view, presumably, was that it preserved the principle that man, as created by God, was intrinsically pure. It also offered an explanation of how sin had (quite literally) 'entered' woman, corrupting humanity as a whole.

Cain fled in a frenzy of fear and guilt, 'a fugitive and a vagabond in the earth', although God now promised him his protection, and 'set a mark' on him, warning that any who harmed him would be punished sevenfold. So the 'mark of Cain', although the sign of an accursed spirit, was at the same time an emblem of God's mercy.

Sons of Seth

And it's at this point that the biblical 'begats' begin: to Cain's son Enoch is born Irad (4, 18):

and Irad begat Mehujael; and Mehujael begat Methusael; and Methusael begat Lamech.

Lamech 'took unto him two wives': one was Adah, the other Zillah. (The scripture seems to take his bigamy in its stride.) The stock of humans, if not perhaps the gene pool, had meanwhile been extended by the birth of another son, Seth, to Adam and Eve – who by now were 130 years old. Seth's son Enos had his own son, Cainan, along with an unspecified

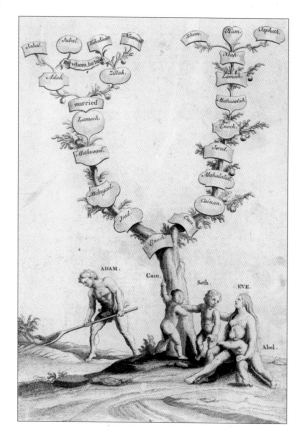

Right: The beginnings of the human family tree: the sons of Cain are shown on the branch to the left; those of Adam and Eve's third son Seth to the right. Abel, of course, was killed before he could become a father.

Left: In the morning of the world's creation, Cain creates the world's first corpse. His murder of his brother Abel may be seen as the inaugurating act of a whole human history of conflict and of crime.

INCESTUOUS ORIGINS

Above: Cain goes into exile with his wife and family. Genesis doesn't dwell on the details, though there's no getting round the fact that, by its own account, Adam's son was married to – and had several children by – his sister.

THE INCEST TABOO, we're told, is universal, and has been so for all known societies – even if the specifics of which relationships have been barred and which accepted may have varied. The Bible sidesteps the issue: 'And Cain knew his wife,' it tells us, without ever naming her; 'and she conceived, and bare Enoch,' it concludes (4, 17).

The midrashic writers weren't so coy, suggesting that both Cain and Abel were born with twin sisters. Twin sisters whom they assumed that they would marry when they came of age. Abel's intended was the more beautiful, one version of the story says: Cain was envious and wanted her for himself. This, the writer claims, was the occasion of the brothers' quarrel. Abel, the stronger, defended himself and, their fight seeming at an end, turned his back on Cain who, taking cowardly advantage, struck and killed him with a stone.

As for the incest question, the midrashim don't engage with this any more than the Book of Genesis does. Different rules applied at the beginning of the world, it seems.

number of other unnamed sons and daughters; Cainan in his turn sired Mahalaleel, whose eldest son was Jared. *He* had a son named Enoch – again, among many others. Enoch's son Lamech had a son named Noah.

Gradually, as all these patriarchs and their anonymous siblings married and had children, the overall population of the earth grew. And growing more wayward and unruly, it would appear. By the time Noah came to manhood, God was thoroughly disenchanted with the human race he had created (6, 5):

And God saw that the wickedness of man was great in the earth, and that every imagination of the thoughts of his heart was only evil continually. And it repented the Lord that he had made man on the earth, and it grieved him at his heart. And the Lord said, I will destroy man whom I have created from the face of the earth; both man, and beast,

Right: Noah and his sons laboured long and hard on the construction of the ark. God gave them detailed instructions on its dimensions, the materials it should be made of and on how exactly it should be built (6, 14).

'The length of the ark shall be three hundred cubits, the breadth of it fifty cubits.'

GENESIS 6, 14

and the creeping thing, and the fowls of the air; for it repenteth me that I have made them.

Fortunately, however, 'Noah found grace in the eyes of the Lord' (6, 8). Although resolved that 'the end of all flesh is come before me' and that the earth was to be destroyed, God decided that the patriarch should be spared.

The World Washed Away

So, God told Noah (6, 14):

Make thee an ark of gopher wood: rooms shalt thou make in the ark, and shall pitch it within and without with pitch. And this is the fashion which thou shalt make it of. The length of the ark shall be three hundred cubits, the breadth of it fifty cubits, and the height of it thirty cubits. A window shalt thou make to the ark … and the door of the ark shalt thou set in the side thereof; with lower, second and third stories shalt thou make it.

Why such a big and solid vessel? 'Behold' (6, 17):

I do bring a flood of waters upon the earth, to destroy all flesh, wherein is the breath of life, from under heaven; and evey thing that is in the earth shall die. But with thee will I establish my covenant; and thou shalt come into the ark, thou, and thy sons, and thy wife, and thy sons' wives with thee.

There was to be hope for animal-kind as well (6, 19):

Right: Filing in two-by-two, the birds and the mammals, the predators and the prey, the boarding of the ark has been re-imagined innumerable times over the centuries. It remains one of scripture's most vividly memorable scenes.

DIVINE DELUGES

'NOAH'S FLOOD', AS specific as its details seem, has much in common with the deluge visited on the Mesopotamian world by the angry gods in the ancient Sumerian *Epic of Gilgamesh*. If it's not too much of a surprise to find similar sounding stories cropping up in the mythologies of neighbouring civilizations. The same might be said for the occurrence of the idea in the Puranas of early India – and even, perhaps, for the story of Deucalion and Pyrrha in Greek tradition. Deucalion and his wife are spared when the earth is otherwise destroyed in a flood sent by an angry Zeus: they build a wooden chest that they stock with provisions to help them through the ordeal.

How, though, are we to account for the fact that floods like this appear in the folklore of a number of Native and South American people?

The obvious answer is the powerful appeal of the idea of the destructive deluge as a symbol. Inevitably, given the appearance of such similar stories across so many different cultures, so geographically remote from one another, some have wondered how merely mythological they are. Could it be that they record a real event? That life on earth *was* cataclysmically disrupted by a genuine deluge in the distant past?

In one sense, of course, it only too obviously was. No scientist seriously doubts that sea levels rose markedly after the end of the last glaciation, around 18,000 years ago. Between about 16,000 and 6000 BCE, the level went up by well over 100m (330ft), radically redrawing the map of world and profoundly shaping the development of those early urbanizing civilizations whose emergence had been made possible by the discovery of agriculture in the 'Holocene'.

A dramatic rise, then – but could it really have been experienced as such when it took place over so many human lifetimes? In the 1990s, geologists William Ryan and Walter Pitman put forward the hypothesis that the Black Sea had been formed by a sudden inundation, following the collapse of a sill of rock and mud, in what is now the Bosporus, in around 6000 BCE. An elegant theory, but with little in the way of reliable evidence to support it – and a great many grounds for scepticism, most geologists believe.

Left: Utnapishtim, the Sumerian 'Noah', thanks the gods for his family's preservation. So widely does the idea of the cleansing world-flood recur in ancient myth that some scholars have suggested that all these stories may just have been based on fact.

And of every living thing of all flesh, two of
every sort shalt thou bring into the ark, to keep
them alive with thee; they shall be male and female.
Of fowls after their kind, and of cattle after their
kind, of every creeping thing of the earth after his
kind, two of every sort shall come unto thee, to keep
them alive. And take thou unto thee of all food that
is eaten, and thou shalt gather it to thee; and it
shall be for food for thee, and for them.

In sparing Noah's family and these animals,
God would 'keep seed alive upon the face of the
earth' (7, 3). Everything else would be destroyed
by 'forty days and forty nights' of heavy rain.

And so it proved:

The waters prevailed, and were increased greatly
upon the earth; and the ark went upon the waters.
And the waters prevailed exceedingly upon the
earth; and all the high hills, that were under the
whole heaven, were covered. Fifteen cubits upward
did the waters prevail; and the mountains were

Above: 'The waters prevailed upon the earth an hundred and
fifty days,' we're told (7, 24). Stocked with examples of every
animal species – including man, of course – the ark was a little
world, afloat in what amounted to a primal chaos.

covered. And all flesh died that moved upon the
earth, both of fowl, and of cattle, and of beast, and
of every creeping thing that creepeth upon the earth,
and every man. All in whose nostrils was the breath
of life, of all that was in the dry land, died. And the
waters prevailed upon the earth an hundred and
fifty days.

We are back where we were at the outset,
then: 'in the beginning', when 'darkness was
upon the face of the deep' (1, 2), and the spirit
of God was moving 'upon the face of the waters'.
This time, though, the emptiness isn't quite
complete. It must have been a nerve-racking
time for Noah and his crew, a mere speck upon
an endless ocean, safely afloat yet still adrift.

> 'He sent forth a raven, which went forth to and fro, until the waters were dried up'.
>
> GENESIS 8, 6

Home and Dry

After 150 days, says Genesis (8, 3), 'the waters were abated':

And the ark rested in the seventh month, on the seventeenth day of the month, upon the mountains of Ararat.

As day followed day, and more and more mountaintops became visible above the waters around him, Noah sent out scouts to see if wider areas were becoming dry (8, 6):

Noah opened the window of the ark which he had made: And he sent forth a raven, which went forth to and fro, until the waters were dried up from the earth. Also he sent forth a dove from him, to see if the waters were abated from off the face of the ground. But the dove found no rest for the sole of her foot, and she returned unto him in to the ark, for the waters were on the face of the whole earth: then he put forth his hand, and took her, and pulled her in unto him into the ark. And he stayed yet other seven days; and again he sent forth the dove out of the ark. And the dove came in to him in the evening, and, lo, in her mouth was an olive leaf pluckt off: so Noah knew that the waters were abated from off the earth. And he stayed yet other

Right: Despairing of the raven, Noah released a dove from the window of the ark to fly out and scout for patches of emerging land. Philip R. Morris (1836–1902) painted this scene in the 'Pre-Raphaelite' style – simple but haunting.

Left: The waters having receded, the ark rests atop Mount Ararat. Drowned bodies litter the hillside. We tend to see the story of the deluge as one of deliverance, of redemption. This engraving doesn't spare us its destructive force.

seven days; and sent forth the dove; which returned not again unto him any more.

Soon, Noah was able to step back on to solid ground with his wife and family. He was able to disembark his animal passengers as well. They set off in their pairs to repopulate the earth. As the human survivors set up altars to offer their thanks to their creator, God announced that he was making a new 'covenant' with Noah and his descendants: no flood would ever again be sent to destroy the earth. He set his bow in the sky – a rainbow – in a token of his faith.

The Curse of Ham

To Noah and his sons, Shem, Ham and Japheth, fell the responsibility for repeopling the earth: 'Be ye fruitful, and multiply; bring

forth abundantly in the earth, and multiply therein' (9, 7). Noah himself, meanwhile, was busy bringing the earth back into cultivation. He established a vineyard – the first one ever known. And, it seems, he made the first wine and became the first man to drink it. He had too much, and collapsed, completely helpless, in his tent. There he lay 'uncovered', in the Bible's words (9, 21), in which condition his son Ham came in and saw him. He went out and told his brothers, who came in and covered up their father's shame.

What, precisely, that shame consisted of – the exact nature of Ham's offence against his father – the account in Genesis doesn't make too clear. All we are told is that the patriarch's younger son 'saw' Noah's nakedness, which hardly seems to justify his rage. When Noah 'awoke from his wine' (9, 24), 'and knew what his younger son

Below: Noah's sons cover their father's nakedness, turning as they do to remonstrate with their brother Ham, who's deemed to have dishonoured him – how is never clear. Ham was held to have condemned his descendants to disgrace and servitude.

BLACK PROPAGANDA

THE RACE THEORY of the nineteenth century, scientific as it was in its pretensions, was happy enough to reach back to the Old Testament for its account of human origins. In this analysis, the human family was divided up into different races, all of them descended from Noah and his three sons. Since Japheth had been 'enlarged' by God (9, 27), it made sense for his descendants – the 'Japhetic' peoples – to be the master race; the whites. Shem's descendants were the Semitic races (not just Jews but Arabs and other Middle-Eastern people).

That left the Hamitic nations – the sons of Ham, condemned to slavery by God, on the authority of the Bible. The suggestion that these were Africans, their skins blackened as a mark of guilt for their ancestor's offence, was debunked as long ago as medieval times, and never advanced even by the more serious proponents of racial 'science' in modern times. As a popular belief, however, and a rationalization of white ownership of African-American slaves, it enjoyed wide acceptance into recent times.

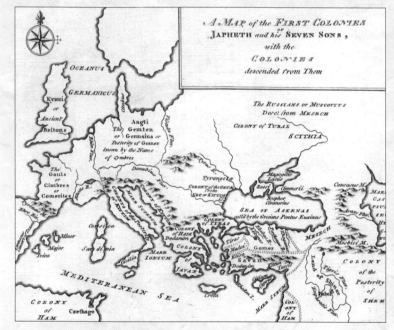

Left: A map of 1760 shows where Japhet's family settled after the nations were 'divided in the earth' (10, 32). It seemed self-evident that the white European nations then enslaving 'Hamitic' Africa could claim descent from the most favoured of Noah's sons.

had done unto him', he cursed his son, and his house of Canaan, to be 'a servant of servants':

God shall enlarge Japheth, and he shall dwell in the tents of Shem; and Canaan shall be his servant.

The apparent disproportionality of this punishment has prompted some scholars to speculate that Ham must have perpetrated some more obviously serious act of sexual dishonour on his father – maybe even rape. Yet, the 'mere' disrespect of seeing Noah's nakedness clearly struck his other two sons as sufficiently serious for them to approach him with their eyes averted ('their faces backward', 9, 23). Either way, it hardly matters: in the ancient subconscious the powers of sight and of sexual possession seem to have been regarded as analogous at some deep

Above: Building frantically – and for what purpose? Human endeavour is intrinsically laudable, but there's a satirical edge to the Babel story: we see the urge to transcend human limitations attended by an overweening ambition to rival God.

level. Hence, in Sophocles' Greek tragedy, King Oedipus gouges out his eyes in symbolic self-castration when he learns that he has unwittingly committed incest with his own mother.

Towering Arrogance

The sons of Noah set out with their wives and families; their children begat more children and within a few generations 'of them was the whole earth overspread' – just as God had wished (9, 19). All were the descendants of a common ancestor, all formed one single culture, 'And the whole earth was of one language, and of one speech' (11, 1). Some settled in the land of Shinar, in the plains of Mesopotamia: as their numbers grew, so did their wealth and

> 'Lord said, Behold, the people is one, and they have all one language'.
>
> GENESIS 11, 3

confidence – and at last their pride. So, they said to one another (11, 3):

Go to, let us make brick, and burn them thoroughly. And they had brick for stone, and slime had they for mortar. And they said, Go to, let us build us a city and a tower, whose top may reach unto heaven; and let us make us a name, lest we be scattered abroad upon the face of the whole earth. And the Lord came down to see the city and the tower, which the children of men builded. And the Lord said, Behold, the people is one, and they have all one language; and this they begin to do; and now nothing will be restrained from them, which they have imagined to do. Go to, let us go down, and there confound their language, that they may not understand one another's speech. So the Lord scattered them abroad from thence upon the face

of all the earth; and they left off to build the city. Therefore is the name of it called Babel; because the Lord did there confound the language of all the earth; and from thence did the Lord scatter them abroad upon the face of all the earth.

Below: Hendrick van Cleve's treatment of the Tower of Babel (1550) seems to have influenced Bruegel's (c. 1563). It's no accident that the Babel story appealed to Renaissance artists, working in an age whose achievements seemed to surpass just about anything that had gone before.

INCEST, INTRIGUE AND INHERITANCE: THE PATRIARCHS

Abraham has traditionally been regarded as the founding father of the Jewish nation, but his was to be a lineage of jealousy, strife and fear.

◆

'I will make of thee a great nation.' GENESIS 12, 2.

Expelled from Eden, Adam and Eve had been forced to step out into an infinitely wider world, full of danger, toil and suffering but also alive with possibilities. God's creation had come full-circle with the Flood: now, from an ark marooned atop a mountain,

Opposite: Jacob, sleeping out one night, saw a ladder reaching to the sky, with angels 'ascending and descending on it' (Genesis 28, 12). 'Jacob's Ladder' may represent the ups and downs of his descendants – and the possibility of salvation in the end.

Noah's descendants had dispersed across the earth. But if humanity's horizons were widening fast, the focus of the Bible was closing in on the 'generations of Shem' – the Semites, or the Jewish people.

Generation succeeded generation, but God did not directly intervene again until Terah had a son named Abram. He took as his wife his half-sister Sarai. This is the first appearance in the Bible of Abraham, the future father of the Jews, although as yet there's no obvious likelihood of his having any sons at all, let alone a nation's worth. 'Sarai was barren,' it seems (Genesis 11, 30): 'she had no child'. Terah took Abram and Sarai, and his other son Haran, and

Left: 'And Terah took Abram his son, and Lot the son of Haran his son's son, and Sarai his daughter in law, his son Abram's wife, and they went forth with them from Ur of the Chaldees' (11, 31).

his son Lot, and they set out from his home city of Ur. They went 'into the land of Canaan' and settled there.

'The Canaanite was then in the land,' we're told, but notwithstanding this the country was given by God to Abram and his descendants:

The Lord appeared to Abram, and said, Unto thy seed will I give this land: and there builded he an altar unto the Lord, who appeared unto him.

'He removed from thence unto a mountain on the east of Bethel,' and there, the Bible tells us, 'he pitched his tent' (12, 8).

Honest Abe?

Even so, Abram's stay in Canaan was to be short: there was 'a famine in the land', so he pressed on towards the south. 'Abram went down into Egypt to sojourn there' (12, 10). Before they arrived, however, he gave his wife a warning:

Behold now, I know that thou art a fair woman to look upon: Therefore it shall come to pass, when the Egyptians shall see thee, that they shall say, This is his wife: and they will kill me, but they will save thee alive. Say, I pray thee, thou art my sister: that it

Below: The Egyptian nobility coveted Sarai's beauty, but she had been warned by her husband to say she was his sister. If this deception saved Abram's life, it did so at some cost, leaving him no excuse to refuse his wife to the lustful Pharaoh.

may be well with me for thy sake; and my soul shall live because of thee.

The patriarch's overriding concern, ungallantly yet understandably, seems to have been for his own safety: this way, should some powerful Egyptian decide to take Sarai for his own wife, he would at least have no motive to murder Abram to make her a widow. The Bible does not report any misgivings – or, for that matter, any reactions at all – on Sarai's part. She kept up the pretence in Egypt as her husband had required.

THE MAN FROM MESOPOTAMIA

IF STORIES LIKE those of the Garden of Eden and Noah's Flood offer intriguing overlaps between the Bible and the myths of other ancient cultures, Abraham's origins in Ur (Genesis 11, 28) represent a fascinating cross-over of the scriptural and archaeological records.

Literally, the land 'in the middle of the rivers', Mesopotamia is the country bordered (roughly) by the Tigris to the east and the Euphrates to the west: this fertile floodplain was the 'cradle of civilization' in the southern part of what is now Iraq. Ur, very much a real city, was an important state in the twenty-first century BCE, a centre of Sumerian power and culture. Extensive excavation at the site since the end of the nineteenth century has uncovered the remains of a big and bustling place, its mud-brick foundations surprisingly well preserved thanks to the aridity of the Iraqi climate.

In the grander scheme of human development, it might be said, Mesopotamia represents the mainstream: here it was that agriculture was developed, cities built and civilization shaped, complete with art and writing. Seen from this perspective, the story of the Jews is a curious sub-plot at best, Abraham's brush with Mesopotamian history his people's proudest moment. Of course, the Jews didn't see it that way – and neither, thanks to the Bible, do we: modernity wouldn't be the same without either story.

Right: Written in the distinctive 'cuneiform' script of successive Mesopotamian civilizations, this tablet records aspects of the administrative life of Ur. The Sumerian city was an important economic, political and cultural centre.

When they arrived in Egypt, it was just as Abram had feared: the Egyptians saw Sarai – and saw that she was 'very fair'.

The princes also of Pharaoh saw her, and commended her before Pharaoh: and the woman was taken into Pharaoh's house. And he entreated Abram well for her sake: and he had sheep, and oxen, and he asses, and menservants, and maidservants, and she asses, and camels. (12, 16).

Abram, in other words, effectively pimped out his wife to Egypt's ruler, although it was the innocent Pharaoh himself who suffered punishment:

And the Lord plagued Pharaoh and his house with great plagues because of Sarai Abram's wife.

The Pharaoh was shocked to discover that Sarai was actually the wife of the foreign visitor: 'What is this that thou hast done unto me?', he asked (12, 18): 'Why didst thou not tell me that she was thy wife? Why saidst thou, She is my sister, so I might have taken her to me to wife?'

Good questions, to which centuries of sympathetic scholarship have struggled to come up with adequate answers. The best that can be said for Abram's lie is that, since Sarai was his half-sister, it was perhaps half-true.

Land and People

No matter. Thanks to his wife's attractions, Abram was 'very rich in cattle, in silver, and in gold' (13, 3) when he and Lot left Egypt for Bethel, back where they'd started. Things weren't quite so easy now. Lot had done well too (we're never told just how), with 'flocks, and herds, and tents' (13, 6):

And the land was not able to bear them, that they might dwell together: for their substance was great … And there was a strife between the herdmen of Abram's cattle and the herdmen of Lot's cattle.

Above: Sarai slinks away from the Pharaoh's palace in disgrace, her true identity and marital status revealed. Successive generations of scholars have been as shocked as the Pharaoh was at Abram's actions, whose logic has never been very clear.

Hence Abram's suggestion that they separate. Lot agreed, and took his family and followers out on to the fertile plains to the east, while Abram remained in the grasslands of Canaan. This was to be his home – and that of his descendants – in perpetuity, the Lord said (13, 15):

Lift up now thine eyes, and look from the place where thou art northward, and southward, and eastward, and westward: For all the land which thou seest, to thee will I give it, and to thy seed for ever. And I will make thy seed as the dust of the earth, so that if a man can number the dust of the earth, then shall thy seed also be numbered. Arise, walk through the land in the length of it and in the breadth of it; for I will give it unto thee.

All this land, and no one to populate it: Sarai's barrenness continued. She did, however, have a handmaid, whose name was Hagar. Egyptian-born, she was, some sources suggest, a princess of the Pharaoh's kingdom. Suffice it to say that she was young and beautiful – a fitting wife for Sarai's husband, it seems she thought (16, 2):

Behold now, the Lord hath restrained me from bearing: I pray thee, go in to my maid; it may be that I may obtain children by her. And Abram hearkened to the voice of Sarai. And Sarai Abram's

Below: Driven out into the desert by an angry Sarai, Hagar receives comfort from an angel sent by God. He tells her to return, put up with her mistress' jealousy, and bear Abram a son: his name will be Ishmael.

wife took Hagar her maid … and gave her to her husband Abram to be his wife.

Trouble and Strife

While it makes no moral judgment on the Patriarch's polygamy, scripture does suggest that the path of bigamous love may not run smooth (16, 4). The stratagem worked, as far as it went: Hagar soon found herself pregnant. Here, however, the trio's trouble started:

When she saw that she had conceived, her mistress was despised in her eyes. And Sarai said unto Abram, My wrong be upon thee: I have given my maid into thy bosom; and when she saw that she had conceived, I was despised in her eyes: the Lord judge between me and thee. But Abram said unto Sarai, Behold, thy maid is in thy hand; do to her as it pleaseth thee.

Not needing to be told a second time, Sarai 'dealt hardly' with her servant and rival, who 'fled from her face'. An angel came upon her cowering by a 'fountain in the wilderness' (16, 7). He told her to go back to her mistress and submit to her authority: she would have a son, and she should name him Ishmael. However difficult the domestic fall-out, Ishmael's birth was gratifying to God, who established a new agreement with Abram (17, 11):

Ye shall circumcise the flesh of your foreskin; and it shall be a token of the covenant betwixt me and you. And he that is eight days old shall be circumcised among you, every man child in your generations.

Not just an agreement, but a new name: 'Neither shall thy name any more be Abram,' the Lord commanded, 'but thy name shall be Abraham, for a father of many nations have I made thee' (17, 5). Sarai too was to be no

Right: A stained-glass window at Klosterneuburg, Austria, shows Abram and Sarah with the infant Isaac. It brings us up with a jolt to think that a few years later, grieved but resolute, the loving father would be preparing to sacrifice his son.

more: she now took the name of 'Sarah' (17, 15), by which she has been remembered by posterity.

Though 90 years old by now, she was to be 'a mother of nations' (17, 16). 'Kings of people shall be of her,' God said. Indeed, he told the astonished Abraham:

'Sarah thy wife shall bear thee a son indeed; and thou shalt call his name Isaac'.

GENESIS 17, 19

Sarah thy wife shall bear thee a son indeed; and thou shalt call his name Isaac: and I will establish my covenant with him for an everlasting covenant, and with his seed after him (17, 19).

To Abraham's plea for God's blessing on the son he already had, God's answer was more ambiguous:

As for Ishmael, I have heard thee: Behold, I have blessed him, and will make him fruitful, and will multiply him exceedingly; twelve princes shall he beget, and I will make him a great nation. But my covenant will I establish with Isaac, which Sarah shall bear unto thee at this set time in the next year (17, 20).

And, far from being assuaged by the birth of an infant of her own, Sarah's jealously only grew. She was angry when one day she saw Ishmael 'mocking' the young Isaac:

She said unto Abraham, Cast out this bondwoman and her son; for the son of this bondwoman shall not be heir with my son, even with Isaac.

Opposite: Far from allaying Sarah's jealousy, the birth of her son Isaac only inflamed it. She had her husband send his mistress Hagar and son Ishmael off into the wilderness. Jean Charles Cazin painted this picture of the pair in 1880.

Sarah's attitude upset Abraham, but God said 'Let it not be grievous in thy sight … for in Isaac shall thy seed be called' (21, 12). Abraham, accordingly, put aside his misgivings and, having provided Hagar and her son with some bread and water, sent them off into the wilderness to fend for themselves.

Sacrificial Son

Scarcely had he lost Ishmael than Abraham had to accept that he was to lose his second son, Isaac, too – and by his own hand, for 'God did tempt him' (22, 1) in a test of loyalty:

And he said, Take now thy son, thine only son Isaac, whom thou lovest, and get thee into the land of Moriah; and offer him there for a burnt offering upon one of the mountains which I will tell thee of.

Heartbroken but unflinching, Abraham rose up, 'saddled his ass, and took two of his young men with him, and Isaac his son, and clave

'A WILD MAN'

'AND HE WILL be a wild man; his hand will be against every man, and every man's hand against him.' The angel's prophecy to Hagar at the well of Beerlahairoi (16, 12) was not auspicious. Even so, Ishmael's birth seems in some way to have moved on the narrative of the Jewish people – in some way to have prompted Sarah's pregnancy.

Although not chosen as father for the Chosen People, Ishmael did found a nation, just as God had promised: by tradition, the Ishmaelites were the ancestors of the Arabs. In some scholarly traditions, indeed, Ishmael – an important prophet of Islam – is seen as having been a direct ancestor of Muhammad.

SODOM AND GOMORRAH

WHILE HE WAS waiting for Sarah to bear his son, Abraham went down to the plains eastward, where his nephew Lot had settled with his people not long before. He'd had his share of difficulties, coming into conflict with a number of local rulers, but emerging victorious in the Battle of the Vale of Siddim (14, 8). Among his enemies there had been the rulers of Sodom and Gomorrah, although this doesn't seem to have been the cause of God's later wrath. Rather, we are told, it was 'because the cry of Sodom and Gomorrah is great, and because their sin is grievous' (18, 20: 'cry' here seems to mean something like 'gossip, rumour or report'). Despite his anger, God agreed to Abraham's plea that he would show mercy on the cities if as few as 50 just men could be found – and even let himself be haggled down to promising clemency if he could find ten.

We're never told what specific sins were committed in the Cities of the Plain – still less is there anything in scripture explicitly to justify the general assumption that the 'Sin of Sodom' was anal sex. There *is* arguably some circumstantial evidence that homosexuality was involved, though. According to Genesis Chapter 19, God sent a pair of angels to the city as his emissaries: scrupulously hospitable, Lot received them in his house. Overnight, however, a crowd of townsmen gathered, surrounding and besieging the house, clamouring for the visitors to be given up to them – that they might 'know' them. Lot, at his wits' end, begged them 'brethren, do not so wickedly' (19, 7):

I have two daughters which have not known man; let me, I pray you, bring them out unto you, and do to them as is good in your eyes: only unto these men do nothing, for therefore came they under the shadow of my roof.

Unmoved, the mob threatened to murder Lot if he continued to resist them. The angels pulled him back inside, and blinded those who hammered on the door.

Next morning, urged on by the angels, Lot took his wife and daughters and fled the city. God warned him: 'Escape for thy life; look not behind thee ... lest thou be consumed' (19, 17):

Then the Lord rained upon Sodom and upon Gomorrah brimstone and fire from the Lord out of heaven; And he overthrew those cities, and all the plain, and all the cities, and that which grew upon the ground.

Forgetting God's awful warning, however, Lot's wife looked back over her shoulder to see what was happening behind them: immediately, 'she became a pillar of salt' (19, 26).

the wood for the burnt offering ... and went unto the place of which God had told him.' Reaching his destination, he told his helpers to wait while he took the wood, ready to make a fire, then led Isaac to the altar and laid him upon it, his knife at the ready.

And Abraham stretched forth his hand, and took the knife to slay his son. And the angel of the Lord called unto him out of heaven, and said, Abraham, Abraham: and he said, Here am I. And he said, Lay not thine hand upon the lad, neither do thou any thing unto him: for now I know that thou fearest God, seeing thou hast not withheld thy son, thine only son from me. And Abraham lifted up his eyes, and looked, and behold behind him a ram caught in a thicket by his horns: and Abraham went and took the ram, and offered him up for a burnt offering in the stead of his son (22, 14).

Sarah died soon after, and Abraham saw this as his cue to find a wife for Isaac, so that ~~might be continued. Travelling to~~ ~~at the city~~

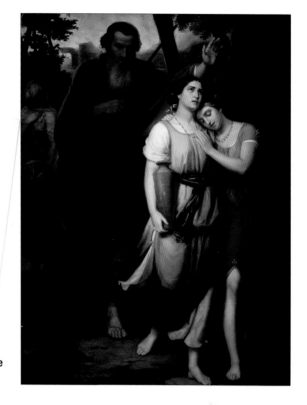

Terrible Twins

Isaac remained in Canaan, happy with his wife. Like Sarah before her, however, Rebekah seemed cursed with barrenness – until, after 20 years, she conceived. It was a difficult pregnancy (25, 22):

> *The children struggled together within her; and she said, If it be so, why am I thus? … And the Lord said unto her, Two nations are in thy womb, and two manner of people shall be separated from thy bowels; and the one people shall be stronger than the other people; and the elder shall serve the younger.*

Opposite: His hand stayed at the final moment, Abraham spares his son Isaac's life after the angel orders him to slay a ram instead (22, 14). By passing this loyalty test, Abraham shows his suitability as patriarch and establishes the loyalty of the Jews.

Above: Brought back to Canaan by her future father-in-law, in this nineteenth-century painting by Vittorio Bianchini, Rebekah first sets eyes on her intended husband Isaac as he walks out to meet them. She likes what she sees, it would appear.

As the boys grew, Esau, the firstborn, revealed himself to be 'a cunning hunter, a man of the field' (25, 27); Jacob 'a plain man, dwelling in tents'. The former was Isaac's favourite – he liked to eat the venison Esau brought home from hunting, but their mother from the first loved Jacob more.

One day, we're told, when Jacob had been boiling up a thick pottage or stew of lentils, 'Esau came from the field, and he was faint' (25, 29). He begged his brother: 'Feed me, I pray thee, with that same red pottage'.

Above: In Guarino da Solofra's *Esau Ceding his Birthright to Jacob* (1642), the startled expression of the boy who serves him his 'mess of pottage' says it all: Esau's reckless attitude allows him to be fleeced by his unscrupulous younger brother.

And Jacob said, Sell me this day thy birthright. And Esau said, Behold, I am at the point to die: and what profit shall this birthright do to me? And Jacob said, Swear to me this day; and he sware unto him: and he sold his birthright unto Jacob. Then Jacob gave Esau bred and pottage of lentiles; and he did eat and drink, and rose up, and went his way (25, 34).

While a modern reader might wonder what sort of sibling loyalty or business ethics the 'Good Book' is encouraging here, the Bible's writers clearly admired the resourceful Jacob over Esau, who 'despised his birthright'.

A Blessing Usurped

Jacob's manoeuvrings didn't stop there: in his undeclared feud with Esau, he had the enthusiastic backing of his mother. Knowing that Isaac, near death, was about to bestow his blessing on his elder son, but had asked Esau first to go out hunting and bring home some of the venison he loved, Rebekah called Jacob, and told him to fetch two kids from his flock of goats. Isaac, old and almost blind, would never realize that this wasn't venison, she reasoned – nor that the son kneeling before him was the wrong one.

Jacob was unconvinced (27, 11):

Esau my brother is a hairy man, and I am a smooth man; My father peradventure will feel me and I shall seem to him as a deceiver; and I shall bring his curse upon me, and not a blessing.

His mother, unperturbed, replied: 'Upon me be thy curse, my son: only obey my voice, and go fetch me them.' Having prepared the kids' meat so that it resembled venison, she used the skins to cover Jacob's hands, and the back of his neck, so that when his father reached out to touch them they felt hairy.

And he came unto his father, and said, My father: and he said, Here am I; who art thou, my son? And Jacob said unto his father, I am Esau thy firstborn; I have done according as thous badest me: arise, I pray thee, sit and eat of my venison, that thy soul may bless me.

Not content with playing fast and loose with the principles of filial piety, Jacob involved God himself in his deception, claiming his direct intervention on his behalf. When Isaac expressed surprise that, if this were truly Esau, he could have been back from his hunt so quickly, Isaac answered: 'Because the Lord thy God brought it to me' (27, 20). That little stumble successfully overcome, the plan continued – working beautifully:

And Isaac said unto Jacob, Come near, I pray thee that I may feel thee, my son, whether thou be my very son Esau or not. And Jacob went hear

Below: The aged, ingenuous Isaac is no match for his scheming wife Rebekah and his younger son Jacob, who has covered his neck and hands with goat-skin to resemble his hairy elder brother. Govert Flinck painted this famous scene in around 1638.

unto Isaac his father; and he felt him, and said, The voice is Jacob's voice, but the hands are the hands of Esau. And he discerned him not, because his hands were hairy, as his brother Esau's hands; so he blessed him.

'Cursed be every one that curseth thee, and blessed be he that blesseth thee'.

GENESIS 27, 27

Asking his son to draw near so he could kiss him, Isaac found any remaining doubts dispelled by the smell of the kidskins in which the young man was draped (27, 27):

See, the smell of my son is as the smell of a field which the Lord hath blessed: Therefore God give

thee of the dew of heaven, and the fatness of the earth, and plenty of corn and wine: Let people serve thee, and nations bow down to thee: be lord over thy brethren, and let thy mother's sons bow down to thee: cursed be every one that curseth thee, and blessed be he that blesseth thee.

Hardly had Jacob left than Esau came back with his venison and begged his father's blessing. Knowing by his voice that it was Esau, Isaac realized what he had done. 'Thy brother came with subtilty,' he said (27, 35), 'and hath taken away thy blessing … Behold, I have made him thy lord, and all his brethren have I given to him for servants; and with corn and wine have I sustained him.' Not surprisingly, Esau swore a cruel vengeance against his brother.

The Trickster Tricked

Fearing for Jacob's life, Rebekah persuaded Isaac to send his second son off to Mesopotamia, to Padan-aram, to stay with Rebekah's brother, Laban, and to work for him. And, it was hoped, to wed one of his daughters. Esau already had two Canaanite wives but, realizing that his father didn't approve of either of them, he went to the house of Isaac's estranged half-brother Ishmael and married Mahalath, his cousin.

Rebekah's plan appeared to be working out. On his arrival in Padan-aram, Jacob saw a beautiful young woman tending sheep: to his delight, he learned that she was Rachel, Laban's daughter. Introduced to her father – his own uncle, of course – Jacob swore to serve Laban for seven years without compensation, except for the promise that he might marry Rachel once his term was done.

Loyally, uncomplainingly, night and day,

Left: Esau's despair on discovering Jacob's treachery was vividly imagined by the English artist William Brassey Hole (1846–1917). All the animal wildness of this hairy, hunting son of nature is apparent as he twists and cries out in his rage.

Above: Jacob declares his love for Rachel, little guessing the length of the courtship he is embarking upon. Laban made him serve him for seven years – and then would only give him Leah; for Rachel he had to serve seven years more.

Jacob worked for his uncle for seven long years until at last he was in a position to claim his prize. To his horror, his uncle led forward Rachel's sister Leah and placed her hand in his. 'It must not be so done in our country, to give the younger before the firstborn,' he explained (27, 26). He *could* have Rachel, Laban said slyly, but that would involve a new and separate deal, and he would have to bind himself to a further seven years' servitude.

The Tables Turned

When that period came to an end, Jacob claimed his wife – the one he'd wanted, Rachel. He also asked his uncle for his wages. Desperate not to lose a herdsman who had managed his cattle and sheep so successfully – increasing them 'unto a multitude' – Laban asked his nephew to name his price. He didn't want money, Jacob said – just any speckled or spotted animals from among Laban's stock. Laban agreed, not realizing that Jacob had no intention of leaving things to genetic chance but had come up with a way of engineering things to his advantage (30, 37), employing the power of visual suggestion:

And Jacob took him rods of green poplar, and of the hazel and chestnut tree; and pilled white strakes in them, and made the white appear which was in the rods. And he set the rods which he had pilled before the flocks in the gutters in the watering troughs when the flocks came to drink, that they should conceive when they came to drink. And the flocks conceived before the rods, and brought forth cattle ringstraked, speckled, and spotted.

Above: Leah looks impassive as an angry Jacob reproaches Laban for giving him the girl, rather than her younger sister Rachel. She lurks in the background, the one that – for now – got away in this representation by Hendrick ter Brugghen (1627).

Not only this, but, we are told (30, 41), Jacob picked out the strongest among Laban's stock for this treatment – disregarding the weaker ones: an early example of selective breeding.

It took Laban and his sons a while to see that, while not technically robbed, perhaps, they had certainly been taken advantage of in no uncertain terms. By the time they realized what had happened, Jacob had fled for his father's home, back in Canaan, along with Rachel and Leah, and the latter's sons. (So far, only the elder woman had borne him children.) And, of course, with abundant flocks and herds of (piebald) livestock.

Laban did catch up with them, but was finally talked round – and even gave his son-in-law his blessing. Resuming his journey, Jacob had reached a place called Penuel or Peniel when he was accosted (32, 24) by a stranger – a man, or an angel – who challenged him to wrestle. All night they struggled and, just before the dawn, the angel broke off their bout and blessed him, telling him 'Thy name shall be called no more

Right: Jacob wrestles with the angel. One of the odder episodes in the Bible, the story (Genesis 32, 24) seems to represent some sort of trial of strength and resolution which Jacob/Israel is deemed to have passed.

Jacob, but Israel: for as a prince hast thou power with God and with men, and hast prevailed.'

The stranger disappeared as the sun came up: the next thing Jacob saw was Esau approaching with his men. The two brothers were once more reconciled. Jacob came back to Canaan and settled at Succoth, near the city of Shalem: he was home again once more, a man of substance.

Jacob and Sons

Jacob had six sons by Leah and a daughter, Dinah, as well – during the lengthy wait for Rachel to conceive – and another two each by Zilpah, who was Leah's handmaiden, and Bilhah, who was Rachel's. But the birth that really thrilled Jacob (now known as 'Israel') was that of Joseph, Rachel's firstborn. He grew up

CHILDLESS MATRIARCHS

SARAH, REBEKAH: BOTH had spent the first years – even decades – of their marriages in barrenness: it was becoming customary in the wives of the patriarchs. Leah, the apparent exception – yielding Jacob no fewer than six sons and a daughter – really just represented an underlining of the rule. Jacob, deceived into taking her as his wife, had only ever accepted her under protest: his real love was for Rachel, who – while being 'beautiful and well favoured' (29, 18) – for so many years could not conceive.

There's a divine perversity at work, it seems: 'And when the Lord saw that Leah was hated, he opened her womb,' says Genesis 29, 31: 'But

Rachel was barren.' Before too long, Rachel is desperate, complaining to her husband (30, 1): 'Give me children, or else I die.' Like Sarah before her, she ends up giving her husband her maidservant to marry – and, just like Hagar, Bilhal conceives at once.

In biblical times – even more than now – the bearing of children was viewed as a vocation: the only real calling, indeed, for the true woman. This near-tradition of childlessness – with final fulfilment – among key women in the Bible amounts to an extended metaphor for the plight of the Jews as a people – always exiled, always awaiting their promised land.

about, and made obeisance to my sheaf. And his brethren said to him, Shalt thou indeed reign over us? Or shalt thou indeed have dominion over us? And they hated him yet the more for his dreams, and for his words.

A second dream drove home the message of the first:

'Behold, the sun and the moon and the eleven stars made obeisance to me.'

If the sun was obviously Joseph's father, and the moon his mother, the 11 stars were the brothers – now incandescent with a jealous rage.

Death to the Dreamer

The brothers' anger took a murderous turn when, tending their flocks in a distant pasture at Dothan, well away from home, they saw their younger brother approaching, sent out to by Israel to join them. 'Behold, this dreamer cometh,' they said (37, 20):

Come now therefore, and let us slay him, and cast him into some pit, and we will say, Some evil beast hath devoured him; and we shall see what will become of his dreams.

But Reuben, the eldest of Jacob's sons, uncomfortable with this conspiracy, persuaded his brothers simply to abandon Joseph in the desert, so that his blood would not be on their hands. At his prompting, they stripped and threw him into the pit without bread or water. Reuben left, on the pretext of telling Jacob that Joseph had been lost: in fact, he was secretly hoping that, once his brothers had left the scene, he could come back, rescue Joseph and restore him to his father.

But he returned to find an empty pit, for, while he was gone, a caravan of Ishmaelite slave-traders had approached the group: seeing them

the apple of his father's eye. The Bible is frank about Jacob's favouritism (37, 3):

'Now Israel loved Joseph more than all his children, because he was the son of his old age: and he made him a coat of many colours.'

Inevitably, this rankled:

And when his brethren saw that their father loved him more than all his brethren, they hated him, and could not speak peaceably unto him.

Joseph's powers as a visionary only vexed them more – especially given that his visions underlined his pre-eminence among them (37, 5):

And Joseph dreamed a dream, and he told it his brethren: and they hated him yet the more. And he said unto them, Hear, I pray you, this dream which I have dreamed: For, behold, we were binding sheaves in the field, and, lo, my sheaf arose, and also stood upright; and, behold, your sheaves stood round

RAPE, RECONCILIATION AND REVENGE

WITH JACOB SETTLED at Succoth, his daughter Dinah set about visiting their new neighbours. She went to Shalem to introduce herself to the ladies of Prince Hamor's household. The Prince's son Shechem saw her there and was seized with desire: 'he took her, and lay with her, and defiled her' (34, 2). Rape, in the ancient world (as it was, indeed, well into modern times), was primarily a crime of property and secondarily of 'honour'. The rights of the woman or girl came a distant third – if they were even recognized at all. Shechem had taken something that belonged to Jacob and his house.

Shechem's love for Dinah was real. Prince Hamor pressed Jacob to let her marry his son – in return, he said, he would give Jacob and his sons whatever they might ask. Answering him 'deceitfully' (34, 13) Jacob's sons insisted that they weren't allowed by religious law to give their sister to a man who had not been circumcised – or even one who came from uncircumcised people:

But in this will we consent unto you: If ye will be as we be, that every male of you be circumcised; Then will we give our daughters unto you, and we will take your daughters to us, and we will dwell with you.

And so it was. Hamor and Shechem agreed to their terms, 'and every male was circumcised' (34, 24).

But two of Jacob's sons, Simeon and Levi, remained unreconciled and – still 'sore' (34, 25) – 'took each man his sword, and came upon the city boldly, and slew all the males.'

They took their sheep, and their oxen, and their asses, and that which was in the city, and that which was in the field, And all their wealth, and all their little ones, and their wives took they captive, and spoiled even all that was in the house.

Below: In revenge for the rape of their sister by Shechem's ruler, Jacob's sons Simeon and Levi, with their followers, fall upon the city and massacre its menfolk, carrying off their women and children to serve them as slaves.

> 'And he knew it, and said, It is
> my son's coat; an evil beast hath
> devoured him'.
>
> GENESIS 37, 31

coming, Judah, the fourth of Jacob's sons, had spoken up:

What profit is it if we slay our brother, and conceal his blood? Come, and let us sell him to the Ishmaelites, and let not our hand be upon him; for he is our brother and our flesh.

The deal was done, and all that remained was for the brothers to cover their tracks (37, 31):

And they took Joseph's coat, and killed a kid of the goats, and dipped the coat in the blood; And they sent the coat of many colours, and they brought it to their father; and said, This have we found: know now whether it be thy son's coat or no. And he knew it, and said, It is my son's coat; an evil beast hath devoured him; Joseph is rent in pieces.

In a frenzy of grief, Jacob tore his clothes 'and put sackcloth upon his loins, and mourned for his son many days' (37, 34) – although Joseph was actually very much alive.

He was, however, in Egypt, where he had been sold into the household of Potiphar, captain of the Pharaoh's palace guard. Here too, he quickly became a favourite (39, 4):

And Joseph found grace in his sight, and he served him: and he made him overseer over his house, and all that he had he put into his hand.

An Amorous Mistress

The special trust he had in Potiphar's house, and the privileged access he enjoyed, were to

Right: Joseph's brothers count their profits as Joseph is carried off by slavers in Konstantin Flavitsky's painting of 1855. Joseph would himself one day have the power to buy and sell them when they journeyed to an Egypt under his effective rule.

bring unfortunate consequences after a time. 'His master's wife cast her eyes upon Joseph,' (39, 7); 'and she said Lie with me.' But Joseph flatly refused to betray his master.

One day, however, when the other servants were out and Potiphar's wife saw Joseph:

She caught him by his garment, saying, Lie with me: and he left his garment in her hand, and fled, and got him out.

What began as bedroom farce took on an uglier aspect entirely when Joseph's mistress, thwarted, cried out that he had tried to rape her. He had fled when she called for help, leaving his garment in her hand, she said (39, 15). Joseph's fall from grace was still more rapid than his rise had been: he was taken from his master's house, and thrown into prison.

Dream Drama

It was not long, however, before Joseph was joined by the Pharaoh's baker and butler. They had fallen foul of their irascible master and had been jailed. Both, in the space of a single night, had strange dreams, and neither could imagine what they had meant. Mentioning the fact to Joseph, he asked them to tell him what they'd seen and offered his own explanation: the Pharaoh was going to think better of his earlier anger with the butler and set him free, he said. As for the baker, his case was very different: within three days he too would be taken from the prison – but only to be put to death, said Joseph.

Opposite: Jacob was inconsolable at the news of his son's 'death'. The coat of many colours – now stained with red blood – seemed to prove it. Jacob tore his own clothes, mourning his son for many days – though Joseph was actually alive and well.

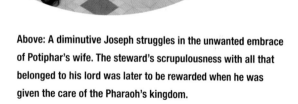

Above: A diminutive Joseph struggles in the unwanted embrace of Potiphar's wife. The steward's scrupulousness with all that belonged to his lord was later to be rewarded when he was given the care of the Pharaoh's kingdom.

Back in the imperial household, and in the Pharaoh's favour, the butler remembered his friend in prison when his master himself reported a pair of perplexing dreams. In the first, he recalled, he was standing by the river when seven 'well favoured' and 'fatfleshed' cows came up out of the water; followed by a further seven, who were 'ill favoured and leanfleshed' (41, 3). The second group ate up the first – at which point the Pharaoh woke up, bemused and seriously unsettled. His second dream did nothing to improve his mood (41, 5):

Behold, seven ears of corn came up upon one stalk, rank and good. And behold, seven thin ears and blasted with the east wind sprung up after them. And the seven thin ears devoured the seven rank and full ears.

Although the Pharaoh sent for all his advisers and magicians, none could tell him what his dream had meant. Then the butler told him of the Hebrew prisoner he had still languishing in jail and how he had successfully interpreted his own – and the baker's – dreams.

Joseph was sent for and told of the Pharaoh's visions: there was no hesitancy in his reply. 'What God is about to do,' he said, 'he sheweth unto the Pharaoh' (41, 28):

Behold, there come seven years of great plenty throughout the land of Egypt; And there shall arise after them seven years of famine; and all the plenty shall be forgotten in the land of Egypt; and the famine shall consume the land.

So severe would the shortage be that it would quite erase the memory of the plenty that had gone before. It was for this reason that the Pharaoh had been sent substantially the same warning twice. God, said Joseph, wanted the

'all the plenty shall be forgotten in the land of Egypt; and the famine shall consume the land'

GENESIS 41, 28

Pharaoh to appoint a 'man discreet and wise' to take charge in Egypt and to confiscate corn in quantity through the good years so that it could be laid up in reserve to see Egypt through its years of famine.

The Pharaoh, much impressed, made Joseph his chancellor: 'See, I have set thee over all the land of Egypt,' he told the sometime slave (41, 42); 'Without thee shall no man lift up his hand or foot' (41, 44).

A Family Reunion

The 'famine was sore in all lands' (41, 57) and Canaan was no exception. Without the benefit of Joseph's guidance, Jacob's household was soon struggling to survive. They had prospered through the good times, and saved money, but hadn't known to lay in the reserves of grain they would need to see them through so harsh and protracted a dearth as they now faced.

Jacob, accordingly, told his sons (42, 2): 'Behold, I have heard that there is corn in Egypt: get you down thither and buy for us from thence; that we may live and not die.' But Benjamin, his youngest son (and Rachel's second – all the dearer to his parents since Joseph's 'death') was to remain with him in Canaan, for Jacob could not bear to lose him.

Joseph, down in the marketplace when his brothers arrived, immediately recognized the

Left: Seven 'well-favoured', 'fatfleshed' cows and then another seven scrawny ones … A medieval-looking Pharaoh has his famous dream: seven 'fat' years of plenteous harvests are to be followed by seven searing years of famine and of want.

Above: His own soothsayers baffled, the Pharaoh has been reduced to hearing the prisoner brought up from his own dungeons. He listens amazed as Joseph deciphers his dream. From that time on, Joseph will be his most trusted adviser.

Canaanites. Even so, he 'made himself strange unto them, and spake roughly unto them' (42, 7). He accused them of being there as spies, come to see 'the nakedness of the land' (42, 9). They insisted that they were an innocent family from Canaan; that they had left behind them an anxious father and their youngest brother. Joseph, unmoved, had the young men arrested: they were lying, he insisted, and would not be freed until they produced this supposed brother.

On the third day, he seemingly relented, allowing them to leave, on condition that they swore to prove their honesty by returning with Benjamin. Not only did Joseph let them take the grain they'd bought: he secreted the money they had paid for it in bags deep in their sacks – as they discovered, to their amazement, on arriving home.

Jacob was furious when he learned of the deal they had struck with the Egyptian official, but simple honesty demanded that they keep to it. Moreover, the appearance of their money at the bottom of their sacks seemed more menacing than reassuring. So the brothers set off again for Egypt, this time with young Benjamin. They were well received, and allowed to buy more grain.

Before they left, however, Joseph hid a precious silver chalice in Benjamin's sack. The brothers set off homeward, entirely unaware. When they were called on to halt by pursuing Egyptian soldiers, they were obviously anxious – the more so when their sacks were searched; but when the chalice was 'found' in Benjamin's, they were stunned.

Frogmarched back to the city, the Canaanites were harangued by the official who, apparently enraged, said that Benjamin would have to hand himself over to serve him as a slave. Judah – the brother behind Joseph's own enslavement – begged that he should stay in Benjamin's place, because their father would not be able to bear the loss of a second favoured son. Joseph, moved despite himself, he forgave his brother there and then. He told his brothers who he was, and asked them to bring their father and family to live with him down in Egypt.

And so it was agreed: Jacob and his whole family made the journey. The house of Israel was once more reunited.

Left: Amidst the opulence of the Egyptian court, a kneeling Judah begs the unyielding official to spare his youngest brother Benjamin, taking him as prisoner in his place. Not for a moment does he realize that he's pleading with another brother, Joseph.

Below: 'I am Joseph; doth my father yet live?' (45, 3). The Pharaoh's official finally reveals his true identity to his brothers and a touching reunion takes place. All past treasons and resentments are forgotten in an outbreak of relief and joy.

III
LAWS AND WARS

It was now that God laid down his laws and gave the Jews his Commandments to live by. There's little evidence that they actually did.

◆

'Thou hast guided them in thy strength.' Exodus 15, 13.

Joseph's family thrived in Egypt. They 'increased abundantly, and multiplied, and waxed exceeding mighty' (Exodus 1, 7). So 'mighty' did they wax (or grow) that 'the land was filled with them'. A new Pharaoh succeeded Joseph's friend, and the prospect he saw was alarming: 'Behold, the people of the children of Israel are more and mightier than we' (1, 9). The Egyptians, accordingly, set about subjecting the immigrants, enslaving them for the construction of 'treasure cities' (1, 11). But

Moses (above) led the Israelites to freedom. Opposite: He hit the floor with his rod and it immediately became a twisting serpent of bronze. He shows it to his followers in this painting by Giuseppi Maria Crespi (lo Spagnuolo), 1690.

the Israelites continued to multiply, and so it went on through generation after generation – no matter how much 'rigour' the Egyptians applied; no matter how 'bitter' they made their lives with their 'hard bondage' (1, 13–14). Finally, one Pharaoh decided that enough was enough and that altogether tougher tactics would have to be used.

Calling the Hebrew midwives to him, he told them that they should kill all boy babies born to their charges; the girls would be allowed to live, to wed Egyptian men. But the women proved recalcitrant: so 'lively' were the Jewish women, they claimed, that they were 'delivered ere the midwives come in unto them' (1, 19). The Pharaoh therefore told his people that they would have to take action themselves, 'saying, Every son that is born ye shall cast into the river, and every daughter ye shall save alive' (1, 22).

Above: 'Every son that is born ye shall cast into the river,' ordered Egypt's Pharaoh. Moses' mother saved her son by literally fulfilling his command. Here she places the infant in a floating cradle in the bulrushes.

Infant Afloat

One woman, a descendant of Joseph's brother Levi, couldn't bear to give her son up for the slaughter. She kept him hidden, managing to do so for three months. As he grew, however, it only became more difficult. So it was that (2, 3):

when she could no longer hide him, she took for him an ark of bulrushes, and daubed it with slime and with pitch, and put the child therein.

Then, we're told, she laid it in the 'flags' (or rushes) by the river's brink. The boy's elder sister stood waiting on the bank nearby to see what would transpire. In the event, no less a figure than the Pharaoh's daughter came

down to wash herself in the Nile and found the basket. 'When she had opened it, she saw the child; and, behold, the babe wept,' (2, 5). Her heart was moved. She guessed that this was 'one of the Hebrews' children', but despite this asked her handmaiden to find her a nurse from among the Jews to mind the child. The boy's sister still being close at hand, the choice naturally fell on her. She brought her brother

up but, as he grew older, she brought him more and more to the Pharaoh's daughter and he 'became her son' (2, 10): 'And she called his name Moses: and she said, Because I drew him out of the water.'

Moses the Murderer

Moses grew up in the royal household but never lost sight of his 'brethren' and their 'burdens' (2, 11). He was appalled one day when he saw an Egyptian hit a Hebrew. 'And he looked this way and that way, and when he saw that there was no man, he slew the Egyptian, and hid him

Below: The Pharaoh's own daughter found the floating baby and 'had compassion on him': 'This is one of the Hebrews' children,' she said. She had a Jewish woman (Moses' own mother) raise him on her behalf.

> "... and he looked, and, behold,
> the bush burned with fire, and
> the bush was not consumed"
>
> EXODUS 3, 2

in the sand' (2, 12). This won him a reputation. Next day, when he saw a fellow Jew hit another in a fight, and remonstrated with him, the man replied (2, 14):

Who made thee a prince and a judge over us? Intendest thou to kill me, as thou killedst the Egyptian?

Not unreasonable questions, in all their insolence – and, as Moses himself wasn't slow to realize, clear evidence that his crime of the day before was now public knowledge.

It was indeed, and it wasn't long before it was known to the Egyptians too, and Moses was forced to flee, a wanted man. He lay low in Midian, a desert region believed by scholars to have been in the northwest of the Arabian peninsula. There he met Reuel (also known as Jethro), a priest of that country, who took him into his house and gave him his daughter Zipporah in marriage (2, 21). She bore him a son, whom they named Gershom, or 'Sojourner', because, said Moses, that was what he himself had been – in his own memorable words (2, 22), 'a stranger in a strange land'.

The Burning Bush

The sojourn looked set to continue, though, and with every appearance of happiness, until – suddenly – Moses received his call from God. The tribulations of his Jewish brethren in their

Left: Moses' place among the Egyptian elite became impossible when, seeing an overseer strike a slave, he attacked the man and killed him, and 'hid him in the sand' (Exodus 2, 12). He was forced to flee into the desert and lie low.

Above: 'Behold, the bush burned with fire, and lo, the bush was not consumed' (3, 3). God spoke to Moses from the burning bush, although Moses 'hid his face', appointing him the leader and the liberator of the Jews.

Egyptian servitude had grown unbearable, 'and they cried, and their cry came up unto God by reason of the bondage' (2, 25):

And God heard their groaning, and God remembered his covenant with Abraham, with Isaac, and with Jacob. And God looked upon the children of Israel, and God had respect unto them.

One day, then, when he was out in the desert looking after his father-in-law's flock, Moses saw a strange sight (3, 2):

The angel of the Lord appeared unto him in a flame of fire out of the midst of a bush: and he looked, and, behold, the bush burned with fire, and the bush was not consumed.

God, the narrative goes on to say, spoke to him 'out of the midst of the bush' (3, 4). (There

MOST POTENT RODS

So ACCUSTOMED ARE we to the idea of Moses as the embodiment of a certain sort of authority – insistently, intimidatingly masculine – that it is a surprise to see how completely out of his depth he feels at first. His immediate response to God's call to patriarchal duty is to feel an overwhelming sense of impotence. So strong are his feelings of inadequacy, indeed, that he's paradoxically almost defiant in his diffidence, repeatedly disputing God's insistence that the Jews will accept his authority.

It doesn't take Sigmund Freud to see the significance of Moses' anxiety – or his rod. 'And the Lord said unto him,' (4, 2): 'What is that in thine hand? And he said, A rod. And he said, Cast it on the ground':

And he cast it on the ground, and it became a serpent; and Moses fled from before it. And the Lord said unto Moses, Put forth thine hand, and take it by the tail. And he put forth his hand, and caught it, and it became a rod in his hand.

A little oddly, it might be thought, the Exodus text makes its first mention of Moses' elder brother Aaron at this point. When Moses expresses anxiety about his lack of the eloquence he'll need to persuade his people, God reminds him that he can always call on Aaron's assistance (4, 14). Aaron (who, we are subsequently to learn, has his own wonder-working rod) is himself a sort of staff or rod in human form. His brother's support and spokesman, 'shall be to thee instead of a mouth' (4, 16), God says, 'And thou shalt take this rod in thine hand, wherewith thou shalt do signs.'

Left: Moses recoils in fear as his staff is transformed into a twisting serpent. God gave him this early version of the 'magic wand' to enable Moses to 'do signs' – often little more than miraculous stunts to impress his followers and enemies.

does seem to be some confusion in these early sections of the Book of Exodus over whether it is Yahweh or his 'angel' who is intervening at any given time.) He told Moses that he had chosen him as his messenger to Pharaoh, 'that thou mayest bring forth my people the children of Israel out of Egypt' (3, 10).

Moses, overwhelmed and overawed, was not convinced that his Jewish brethren would accept his authority – let alone that Egypt's Pharaoh would meekly accept the removal of his slaves. God gave him his promise that the Jews would 'hearken' to his voice, adding that he would, with Moses' assistance, bring his people out of their affliction 'unto a land flowing with milk and honey' (3, 17). As for Pharaoh, what Moses said was true, said God: 'I am sure that the king of Egypt will not let you go, no, not by a mighty hand' (3, 19). For this reason, he said, he would 'smite Egypt with all my wonders' (3, 20).

An Unfavourable Pharaoh

Making his way with his family into the land of Egypt, Moses was surprised to meet Aaron in the wilderness. God had ordered him to await his brother there (4, 27). The two went together to the Pharaoh's palace and, undaunted now, addressed the Egyptian ruler (5, 1):

A NEGLECTFUL FATHER?

ONE OF THE stranger, more unaccountable incidents in this early part of the Bible occurs when Moses and Zipporah are making their way to Egypt with their son Gershom and put up at an inn. There, we are told (4, 24), the Lord met Moses, 'and sought to kill him'. No direct explanation is given for this assault by God on his own chosen representative, although Zipporah's prompt action presumably holds the answer. She, we are told (4, 25), 'took a sharp stone, and cut off the foreskin of her son'. Casting it at Moses' feet, she said, 'Surely a bloody husband art thou to me.'

It isn't clear whether Moses' is literally bloody, caught in the spray from his son's crude circumcision, or 'bloody' in some other, more metaphorical way. It had of course been a condition of God's covenant with Abraham that he should not only be circumcised himself but that 'he that is eight days old shall be circumcised among you, every man child in your generations' . The interest Moses had maintained in his mother's people as he grew up should surely have meant that he understood

the importance of this custom – although if God had been that angry at his neglect, why had he chosen him as his representative in the first place?

Right: Moses, Zipporah and Gershom sit with Jethro in a tableau of togetherness without a hint of the drama to come. Zipporah's act in circumcising her son to save her 'bloody husband' showed the importance of the ritual for the Jews.

Thus saith the Lord God of Israel, Let my people go, that they may hold a feast unto me in the wilderness. And Pharaoh said, Who is the Lord, that I should obey his voice to let Israel go. And they said, The God of the Hebrews hath met with us; let us go, we pray thee, three days' journey into the desert and sacrifice unto the Lord our God.

Pharaoh did not see why he should release the Jews from their 'burdens' for this long. On the contrary, irritated by these demands, he ordered his overseers to work their charges harder. Descending into pettiness, he told his 'taskmasters' to take away the straw the slaves needed in their work to make mud bricks bind properly together: they would either have to go out and gather more straw on their own time or do without.

Inevitably, the order caused confrontations between the frustrated workforce and their overseers. The slaves downed tools and were beaten for their pains. As inevitably (and as, surely, the Pharaoh had anticipated), it was Moses and Aaron who ended up being blamed.

Since I came to Pharaoh to speak in thy name, he hath done evil to this people; neither hast thou delivered thy people at all?

Promises and Plagues

'Now', said the Lord (6, 1), 'shalt thou see what I will do to Pharaoh.' And so they did, starting with a divine attack on the water

Below: The Egyptians well understood the potent symbolism of the serpent – hence the uraeus: the rearing cobra on the Pharaoh's crown. The transformation of Aaron's rod was not just a frightening trick but an audacious defiance of Egyptian power.

supplies on which Egypt so depended. On God's instructions, Moses told Aaron to hold out his rod 'upon the waters of Egypt, upon their streams, upon their rivers, and upon their ponds' (7, 19). Aaron carried out his brother's bidding and, immediately, 'in the sight of Pharaoh, and in the sight of his servants':

All the waters that were in the river were turned to blood. And the fish that was in the river died; and the river stank, and the Egyptians could not drink of the water of the river; and there was blood throughout all the land of Egypt (7, 21).

Far from being intimidated, however, the 'Pharaoh's heart was hardened, neither did he hearken unto them; as the Lord had said' (7, 22). Egypt spent a profoundly uncomfortable

Above: The apocalypse comes early for Pharaonic Egypt, in a scene imagined by the English artist John Martin (1789–1854): people rush about in panic at the sight of the River Nile running red with blood.

week without water, but there was no sign whatsoever of any easing in the sufferings of Israel.

Next, then, the Lord told Moses he must threaten Pharaoh with another plague. 'The river shall bring forth frogs abundantly,' he should warn him (8, 3):

which shall go up and come into thine house, and into thy bedchamber, and upon thy bed, and into the house of thy servants, and upon thy people, and into thine ovens, and into thy kneading troughs…

Exodus. 8.

Above: Frogs don't seem so threatening compared with some of the other Plagues of Egypt. But this engraving – created by Matthäus Merian for his *Illustrated Bible* (c. 1627) – points up the peculiarly personal repugnance of seeing them everywhere.

Frogs everywhere, in other words. And so it proved. At the command of Moses, Aaron again stretched out his rod over the rivers, streams and ponds: this time, though, the water remained unchanged. It was what emerged from it that seemed so shocking: frogs in their millions – till the whole country was carpeted in their green, gold, wriggling, hopping forms.

Enough was enough, the Pharaoh decided: calling for Moses and Aaron he asked them to get their God to take the frogs away – and I will let the people go' (8, 8). This concession won, God kept his side of the bargain:

And the frogs died out of the houses, out of the villages, and out of the fields. And they gathered them together upon heaps; and the land stank.

However, when the Pharaoh saw that the plague had gone, he started to wonder why he'd made concessions. Instead, he 'hardened his heart and harkened not unto them' (8, 15).

One Thing After Another

Next it was the turn of the lice. At God's commandment, Aaron struck the dust with his rod, 'and it became lice in man, and in beast;

all the dust of the land became lice throughout all the land of Egypt'. Still loath to concede, the Pharaoh called upon his sorcerers to rid him of this new plague, but for all their formidable powers they could not. 'This', they told their master, was 'the finger of God', and by no means effectively to be resisted, but the Pharaoh was in no mood to hear reason – even from magicians.

While all Egypt itched and scratched, then, the Pharaoh remained utterly obdurate – even when a fourth plague, this one of flies, ensued. Perhaps the most unpleasant yet, it afflicted not just the royal palace but every dwelling in the country: all were abuzz with swarms of busy flies. Every surface became coated with a

Below: The Hebrew 'arob ('swarm') in Exodus posed problems from the start. Whilst Christian interpreters tended to assume that the Fourth Plague of Egypt was of flies, earlier Jewish scholars imagined vaguer but more exotic 'noxious beasts'.

heaving, milling mass; they clustered around every item of food and flew into people's eyes, up their noses and even into their mouths.

> ## 'And the frogs died out of the houses, out of the villages, and out of the fields.'
>
> EXODUS 8, 13

Once more, after apparently faltering and offering concessions, Pharaoh reneged as soon as the plague had abated. This time, then, God sent down a 'very grievous murrain' (9, 3) – some unspecified cattle disease – upon the country's herds. The news that the livestock of the Jews had been left untouched was a shock to the Pharaoh. Yet again, though, the consequence

Plate IV.

Exod. IX. Ver. 23 _The Lord sent Thunder, &c._

The Plague, of Thunder, and Hail

Above: Like a puppetmaster, God directs the actions of his mortal representative, Moses, as he unleashes the Plague of Locusts on Egypt's green and fertile land. A coloured woodcut from the fifteenth-century Nuremberg Bible.

was merely that his heart was hardened, and that 'he did not let the people go'.

From Lesions to Locusts

And so, God said to Moses and Aaron (9, 8):

Take to you handfuls of ashes of the furnace, and let Moses sprinkle it toward the heaven in the sight of Pharaoh. And it shall become small dust in all the land of Egypt, and shall be a boil breaking forth with blains upon man, and upon beast, throughout all the land of Egypt.

This proved the most potent plague so far: the Pharaoh called his sorcerers to see off the affliction, but they were completely helpless (9, 11): 'The magicians could not stand

Left: 'The hail smote throughout all the land of Egypt all that was in the field, both man and beast; and the hail smote every herb of the field, and brake every tree of the field' (9, 25).

before Moses because of the boils; for the boil was upon the magicians, and upon all the Egyptians.'

After the boils came 'a very grievous hail' (9, 18), the like of which had never before been seen in Egypt. But this was not the worst of it, for 'fire mingled with the hail': the crops were flattened; the trees snapped and the livestock killed in the fields by the violence of its impact.

Once again, the Pharaoh folded: 'I have sinned this time: the Lord is righteous,' he acknowledged:

and I and my people are wicked. Intreat the Lord (for it is enough) that there be no more mighty thunderings and hail and I will let you go.

As previously, however, his penitence didn't outlast the passing of the plague. As soon as the storms had ceased, he changed his mind again.

Now, then, God sent locusts – their unimaginable swarming darkening the sky still more completely than the stormclouds of the previous plague.

'They covered the face of the whole earth,' we're told (10, 15):

so that the land was darkened; and they did eat every herb of the land, and all the fruit of the trees which the hail had left: and there remained not any green thing in the trees, or in the herbs of the field, through all the land of Egypt.

Again, the Pharaoh begged forgiveness and promised Moses that he would immediately free his people if he'd only lift this affliction

Below: Materially the most trivial of the Plagues, perhaps, but psychologically terrifying, three days of darkness disorientated the Egyptians completely; gave them the sense that the normal order of their days, their lives, had been abandoned.

– and yet again he immediately went back on his word. A plague of three days' total darkness didn't convince him to issue anything more than his now-familiar empty show of compliance with God's will, so at last the Lord was provoked to bring down upon the Pharaoh and his Egyptian people a plague of a much more cruel kind.

Punishment and Passover

Sending Moses off to warn his people to get together, beg or borrow all the jewellery and valuables they could find, and prepare for an abrupt departure, he promised to unleash a chastisement Pharaoh wouldn't have the heart to fight. 'About midnight,' he told Moses (11, 4):

will I go out into the midst of Egypt: And all the firstborn in the land of Egypt shall die, from the firstborn of the maidservant that is behind the mill; and all the firstborn of beasts. And there shall be a great cry throughout all the land of Egypt, such as

Above: 'There shall be a great cry throughout all the land of Egypt' (11, 6). With the Tenth Plague, God at last hit the Pharaoh where he really hurt. The Smiting of the Firstborn finally precipitated the Israelites' departure.

there was none like it, nor shall be like it any more. But against any of the children of Israel shall not a dog move his tongue, against man or beast; that ye may know how that the Lord doth put a difference between the Egyptians and Israel.

On God's instructions, the Jewish families had marked their doors with lamb's blood. That way he (or his avenging angel: the scripture isn't clear) knew to 'pass over' their houses and leave them safe. In other Egyptian homes, however, it was a different story (12, 29):

And it came to pass, that at midnight the Lord smote all the firstborn in the land of Egypt, from the firstborn of Pharaoh that sat on his throne unto the firstborn of the captive that was in the dungeon; and all the firstborn of cattle. And Pharaoh rose up in the night, he, and all his servants, and all the Egyptians; and there was a great cry in Egypt; for there was not a house where there was not one dead.

Amid all this confusion, God told Moses and Aaron to call their people together, telling them to take their flocks and herds and make their getaway. The ordinary Egyptians saw what they were doing, but – far from attempting to stop them – they were 'urgent upon' them to be 'out of the land in haste' (12, 33), for if the Israelites stayed, they reasoned, 'We be all dead men.'

A NEW TRADITION

THE SLAUGHTER OF the Egyptians' firstborn and – more to the point – the sparing of the Children of Israel's children was, God told Moses, to be a sort of fresh start for the Jewish people (12, 2). 'This month shall be unto you the beginning of months; it shall be the first month of the year to you.'

On its tenth day, they should gather together in their houses, families and neighbours, to make a feast of a chosen lamb – 'without blemish, a male of the first year' (12, 5). They should keep this alive until the evening of the fourteenth day, at which point it should be killed before the assembled company, some of its blood being used to mark 'the two side posts and … the upper door post of the houses, wherein they shall eat it' (12, 7). That very night, the lamb should be roasted in the fire before being eaten with unleavened bread and 'bitter herbs' (12, 8). No leftovers were to be put by, and that of the animal that did remain uneaten the next morning should be destroyed by burning in the fire.

They were to eat as if they were about to set out on a journey – as indeed they were. They should eat it:

with your loins girded, your shoes on your feet, and your staff in your hand; and ye shall eat it in haste: it is the Lord's passover. For I will pass through the land of Egypt this night, and will smite all the firstborn in the land of Egypt, both man and beast; and against all the gods of Egypt I will execute judgment: I am the Lord.

The lamb's blood on their doorposts would be a 'token' or a signal to the Lord (12, 13): 'When I see the blood, I will pass over you, and the plague shall not be upon you to destroy you, when I smite the land of Egypt.'

Thenceforth, God said, he wished them to keep this day as a 'memorial … ye shall keep it a feast to the Lord throughout your generations.'

Above: A father marks the door of his home with the blood of the sacrificial lamb, saving his family from God's anger. It would also initiate a ritual tradition lasting centuries: Passover remains one of the most important Jewish festivals.

Into the Wilderness

So, the children of Israel set out, 'about six hundred thousand on foot that were men, beside children … and flocks, and herds, even very much cattle' (12, 37). Such was the haste with which they left that, for food on the march, 'they baked unleavened cakes of the dough which they brought forth out of Egypt' (12, 39): there simply hadn't been time to use yeast and allow the dough to rise. With God to guide them, though, they made good speed (13, 21): 'The Lord went before them by day in a pillar of cloud, to lead them the way; and by night in a pillar of fire, to give them light.'

Their hurry was all too justified. It wasn't long before the Pharaoh realized what had happened and regretted the passivity with which he'd let Moses and his people leave. And, we're told (14, 6):

he made ready his chariot, and took his people with him. And he took six hundred chosen chariots, and all the chariots of Egypt, and captains over every one of them.

The Egyptian army mobilized, the Pharaoh set off in hot pursuit.

They caught up with the fugitives near the shores of the Red Sea. The children of Israel, understandably, were 'sore afraid'. Trapped as they were, with the deep waters before them and the angry Egyptians behind, they took out their anxieties on Moses, the apparent author of their present danger. 'Because there were no graves in Egypt,' they asked him (14, 11), 'hast thou taken us away to die in the wilderness?'

A Way Through the Water

But Moses, with God's backing, told them that they were not to fear. Instead, they watched awestruck, while he 'stretched out his hand over the sea' (14, 21):

And the Lord caused the sea to go back by a strong east wind all that night, and made the sea dry land, and the waters were a wall unto them on their right hand, and on their left.

Below: The Red Sea parts, at Moses' command, so he can lead his people through to freedom, a moment of huge symbolic significance in the Jewish story. The scene is imagined here by Vasilii Alexandrovich Kotarbinsky (1849–1921).

So, with Moses and Aaron leading them, the children of Israel set off across the strip of seabed that, by God's miraculous power, had opened up before them. Even now, the

> ### 'And the waters returned, and covered the chariots, and the horsemen ...'
> EXODUS 14, 28

Egyptians wouldn't give up their pursuit: they drove their chariots down across the shore and into the muddy corridor between the waves. They were not going to let the children of Israel slip so easily from their grasp.

God was watching from heaven, though, 'through the pillar of fire and of the cloud' (14, 24), and he was not going to allow his people to be caught and killed. He took the wheels from the Egyptians' chariots (14, 25), 'that they drave them heavily', then, as the Egyptian generals decided that it was perhaps time to turn and flee, he told Moses once again to raise his hand over the waters:

And the waters returned, and covered the chariots, and the horsemen, and all the host of Pharaoh that came into the sea after them: there remained not so much as one of them (14, 28).

But the children of Israel emerged unscathed, euphoric – and finally convinced of the greatness of their God. Miriam, the prophetess – the sister of Moses and Aaron – took up a timbrel (a small hand-drum), we are told (15, 20): 'and all the women went after her with timbrels and with dances.' As the people exulted

Right: As the last of the Israelites make it safely ashore, the pursuing army of the Pharaoh is engulfed by the rising Red Sea waters. The German artist Lucas Cranach the Elder painted this picture in 1530.

in their deliverance, Miriam led them in their celebrations: 'Sing ye to the Lord,' she cried (15, 21), 'for he hath triumphed gloriously.'

An Arid Shore

The jubilation was short-lived. Had they avoided drowning only to die of thirst? 'They went three days in the wilderness, and found no water' (15, 22). Reaching one oasis, at a place called Marah, they went down excitedly to drink, but found

its waters far too bitter for human consumption (15, 24). Again, the people turned on Moses. Fortunately, God told him of a tree whose wood, when thrown into the water, made it sweet.

Eastward they journeyed, past the wells of Elim and on into the 'wilderness of Sin'. Not an allegorical name, or a metaphor of any kind, but a geographical location (albeit now uncertain, but apparently somewhere between the oasis settlement of Elim and the Sinai).

Opposite: 'I will rain bread from heaven for you,' said God (16, 4) to a desperate Moses, and so he did. In this fifteenth-century painting we see the joyous Israelites collecting the miraculous manna as it falls.

Below: Moses strikes the barren rock and water gushes forth – a godsend for the Israelites. They would have been too thirsty to contemplate the wider symbolic implications, though in hindsight the suggestion of phallic fertility can't easily be ignored.

Food was running low, and the children of Israel were restive. 'Behold,' said the Lord to Moses (16, 4), 'I will rain bread from heaven for you.' And, he added, 'at even' – that is, in the evening – 'ye shall eat flesh' (16, 12):

And it came to pass, that at even the quails came up, and covered the camp; and in the morning the dew lay round about the host. And when the dew that lay was gone up, behold, upon the face of the wilderness there lay a small round thing, as small as the hoar frost on the ground. And when the children of Israel saw it, they said one to another, It is manna: for they wist not what it was. And Moses said unto them, this is the bread which the Lord hath given you to eat.

Scholars have speculated for centuries over what this 'manna' might have been: the silky froth from a seedpod of some desert plant; the secretions from some insect; some fibrous fungus. Others have been happy enough to accept that this really was just 'manna from heaven' – a miraculous and utterly unaccountable gift from God. Either way, it was to save their lives, not just now but in the rest of their wanderings: they were, says Exodus, to eat manna as their staple for the next 40 years.

Water was always a problem. One day, when once again the children of Israel were growing restive and resentful, God told Moses to take his rod and strike a rock he showed him. Before the watching Israelites, Moses struck the stone and water came streaming forth (17, 6). Another sign of God's favour towards his chosen people.

Showdown on Sinai

In the meantime, they pressed on into Midian, where Moses was reunited with Jethro, his father-in-law (18, 70), who advised him on setting up a hierarchy of leaders through which to rule what was now a big and potentially wayward nation. Soon after – in the third month after their first flight from their Egyptian bondage – they found their way into the Sinai desert. They made camp at the foot of Mount Sinai. 'On the third day, in the morning', the Book of Exodus tells us (19, 16):

There were thunders and lightnings, and a thick cloud upon the mount, and the voice of the trumpet exceeding loud; so that all the people that was in the camp trembled.

Moses lined his people up at the bottom of the mountain while the trumpet blast grew louder. Some portentous moment was clearly impending:

Mount Sinai was altogether on a smoke, because the Lord descended upon it in fire: and the smoke thereof ascended as the smoke of a furnace, and the whole mount quaked greatly (19, 18).

Hence the suggestion by some scholars that an actual volcanic eruption may have been taking place, though this seems an unnecessarily literal-minded view of what are surely more convincingly seen as the seismic stage effects

A CODE FOR LIVING

THE BIBLE DOESN'T at this point give God's injunctions any special name – the title 'Ten Commandments' comes later, at Deuteronomy 5, 4. They're not even presented as a list here – although a few more snappy 'Thou shalts' do take this form. The early ones are positively wordy in the justifications they offer for themselves: they're as much explanations as they are commandments.

It's important, in this context, to remember just how unfamiliar – even counterintuitive – the idea of monotheism would have been to an ancient people like the earliest Jews. The first four commandments (so almost half the total) in their different ways are all concerned with ensuring that the believer will give God his due. Only then does the 'Decalogue' address those sorts of rulings that the modern reader might have expected to come first: those that facilitate the smoother (and, of course, more ethical) running of human society.

- *I am the Lord thy God, which have brought thee out of the land of Egypt, out of the house of bondage. Thou shalt have no other gods before me.*
- *Thou shalt not make unto thee any graven image, or any likeness of any thing that is in heaven above, or that is in the earth beneath …*
- *Thou shalt not take the name of the Lord thy God in vain …'*
- *Remember the sabbath day, to keep it holy. Six days shalt thou labour, and do all thy work. But the seventh day is the sabbath of the Lord thy God: in it thou shalt not do any work, thou, nor thy son, nor thy daughter, thy manservant, nor thy maidservant … For in six days the Lord made heaven and earth, the sea, and all that in them is, and rested the seventh day.*
- *Honour thy father and thy mother.*
- *Thou shalt not kill.*
- *Thou shalt not commit adultery.*
- *Thou shalt not steal.*
- *Thou shalt not bear false witness against thy neighbour.*
- *Thou shalt not covet thy neighbour's wife, nor his manservant, nor his maidservant, nor his ox, nor his ass, nor any thing that is thy neighbour's.*

> 'And he took the calf which they had made, and burnt it in the fire.'
>
> EXODUS 32, 20

appropriate to a divinity's descent to earth. 'And the Lord came down upon Mount Sinai,' the account continues, 'and the Lord called Moses up to the top of the mount.' He stayed there for 40 days and nights while God gave him the rules he wanted the Jewish people to make the centre of their moral lives. He also gave him detailed instructions as to the offerings that were to be made to him, as well as (in chapters 25–6) the Ark of Covenant in which his sacred treasures were to be carried while they were on the march, and the Tabernacle or tent – a sort of travelling temple – they were to construct.

The Golden Calf

Exodus hasn't so far painted a particularly impressive portrait of the Chosen People. The 'Children of Israel' seem children indeed –

THE SMALL PRINT

THE TEN COMMANDMENTS are really no more than a summary of the scores of orders that, according to Exodus, God gave Moses in the course of their confabulation atop Mount Sinai. While some of these simply reiterate the contents of the Commandments, perhaps spelling out the appropriate punishments – 'And he that curseth his father, or his mother, shall surely be put to death' (21, 17) – others help fill out the detail of what ultimately amounts to something like a comprehensive code of law.

Encountered now, over 2000 years on, many of course seem culturally alien. Often, it's the specificity of the order that takes us aback. 'If fire break out, and catch in thorns, so that the stacks of corn, or the standing corn, or the field, be consumed therewith; he that kindled the fire shall surely make restitution.'

Many 'make sense' to us – at least at the instinctive level. Whatever our views on capital punishment in the modern-day context, for example, most of us can relate to the revulsion underlining the rule that 'Whosoever lieth with a beast shall surely be put to death' (22, 19). If we're liable to be less comfortable with the command that 'Thou shalt not suffer a witch to live' (22, 18), we can at least recognize that historically people have often lived haunted by genuine terror of the powers of witchcraft, and that these fears have often been reflected in cruel punishments.

Sometimes, a stricture that begins by seeming pleasingly humane can take an unexpected turn. It seems only fitting, for example, to see that a master who hits and kills his servant should suffer punishment (21, 20) – that, if the servant survives, he should remain unscathed because he or she is his master's property, not so much (21, 21). Likewise, the ruling that a thief should have to make restitution for what he steals seems admirably sensible. But it's a shock to see that, if he can't afford to give that restitution, the cost should be made up from his own sale into slavery (22, 2).

Above: The Jews availed themselves of Moses' absence on Mount Sinai by making Aaron create a golden calf for them to worship. Such relapses into paganism recur regularly in the Old Testament, reminding us how new the idea of monotheism was.

whiny and resentful in their attitudes to Moses, the man who'd given them leadership in their escape from Egypt; ungrateful towards the God who's rescued them. Why would they be different now?

Descending from the mountain after his lengthy meeting with God, Moses arrived at his people's camp to find that they'd spent the time growing disenchanted with his leadership – and, more damagingly, with the authority of God. While their creator had been warning Moses against the necessity of avoiding 'graven images', they had been bullying his brother Aaron into making them idols – gods they could follow in Moses' place. Reluctantly, he had complied, collecting all the gold they had about them – in earrings and other jewellery – and melting it down to make a grandiose 'god', a golden calf.

Moses, coming down the mountain bearing God's Commandments, set in tablets of stone, saw his people chanting and singing around this monstrous statue (32, 19). Throwing down the tablets in disgust, he broke them – but the calf he 'burnt … in the fire, and ground it to powder, and strawed it upon the water, and made the children of Israel drink of it' (32, 20). He had

Left: As imagined by the French engraver Gustave Doré in 1866, a furious Moses smashes the stone tablets containing the ten commandments that God has given him. God's law prevails, but the tablets are broken and (symbolically) have to be renewed.

the people build their Tabernacle, as God had demanded, and expiate their guilt for a rebellion that may in hindsight be seen symbolically as that last inglorious fling with paganism that was to confirm the Jews in their adherence to the Laws of Moses and their God.

Keeping it Clean

The Book of Leviticus describes the rules laid down by God for the sort of ritual offerings that were to be made in the Tabernacle and the rules that were to govern the lives of the Jews and of their priests. Many of Leviticus' strictures simply echo rulings we already encountered in the Book of Exodus. Often, though, there is more detail here. Here, then, along with prescriptions for worship, are the taboos to be observed in eating: 'All that have not fins and scales in the seas, and in the rivers' (11, 10); 'the vulture, and the kite after his kind … the little owl, the cormorant, and the great owl' (11, 14), for example. More famously, there is the prohibition against 'the carcases of every beast which divideth the hoof, and is not clovenfooted, nor cheweth the cud' (11, 27). Even carrying such carcases was a source of

Below: A sort of proto-temple, erected by the Israelites on Moses' instructions to provide a cover for the Ark of Covenant and for all its attendant rites, the original Tabernacle was – quite literally – a tent.

deep uncleanness. Other marks of uncleanness were the sores that stemmed from diseases such as leprosy. Leviticus goes into great detail about how the potential contamination from sufferers was to be contained. Women, Eve's successors, were another potent source of impurity. Even so, they were deemed still more unclean at some times than at others (15, 19):

And if a woman have an issue, and her issue in her flesh be blood, she shall be put apart seven days: and whosoever toucheth her shall be unclean until the even. And every thing that she lieth upon in her separation shall be unclean; every thing also that she sitteth upon shall be unclean. And whosoever

Above: This fragment of Leviticus from an ancient Torah scroll was found by a Bedouin herdsman in a cave at Nahal Arugot, in the West Bank, in 2004. It dates from the time of the last Jewish revolt against Roman rule, c. 135 BCE.

MISMATCHED RELATIONSHIPS

LEVITICUS 18, 22 is often cited as the definitive biblical prohibition on homosexuality – and it's true, the passage doesn't leave much room for doubt:

Thou shalt not lie with mankind, as with womankind; it is abomination.

No mention is made of womankind lying with womankind, although some of those modern Christians who are so determined that we take the prohibition on male homosexuality at literal face-value would have us read this verse more figuratively in ruling out lesbian relations too.

Just to be absolutely clear, Leviticus follows up with a reiteration in chapter 20, verse 13:

If a man also lie with mankind, as he lieth with a woman, both of them have committed an abomination; they shall surely be put to death; their blood shall be upon them.

But then, as liberal commentators have gleefully reminded us in recent years, Leviticus is uncompromising in its condemnation of the eating of shellfish – without having mobilized any great crusade by the Christian Right. As for what it sees as mismatched relations, it has something of a mania on this theme (19, 19):

Thou shalt not let thy cattle gender with a diverse kind: thou shalt not sow thy field with mingled seed; neither shall garment mingled of linen and woollen come upon thee.

off from among their people.

All purity, perhaps, was ultimately moral. Leviticus is unforgiving in its attitude to adultery, for example, going well beyond the 'Thou shalt not ...' of the Exodus commandment (20, 10):

And the man that committeth adultery with another man's wife, even he that committeth adultery with his neighbour's wife, the adulterer and the adulteress shall surely be put to death.

Priestly Prohibitions

These prohibitions were still more important for the priestly class, who were supposed to lead society by example. Some of the rules that bound them seem unfathomable now:

toucheth any thing that she sat upon shall wash his clothes, and bathe himself in water, and be unclean until the even.

The man who touched a woman in such a state might be deemed 'unclean until the even', but if he had sexual relations with her he had rendered himself unfit for society (20, 18):

And if a man shall lie with a woman having her sickness, and shall uncover her nakedness; he hath discovered her fountain, and she hath uncovered the fountain of her blood; and both of them shall be cut

They shall not make baldness upon their head, neither shall they shave off the corner of their beard. (21, 5)

Others, like the laws against men with physical imperfection approaching the altar – 'a blind man, or a lame, or he that hath a flat nose ... that is brokenfooted, or brokenhanded, or crookbackt, or a dwarf, or that hath a blemish in his eye ...' (21, 18) – seem cruelly discriminatory to us now, even if they do still make a recognizable sort of symbolic sense.

Above: 'I am the Lord thy God, which hath brought thee out of the land of Egypt ...' God's deliverance of the Jews from bondage was key to his authority and that of the law he laid down: here Moses leads his people through the wilderness.

(Out of respect for God's greatness, he should be ministered to only by the most flawless of his human creation.)

It goes without saying that priests were to make their marriages and conduct their sexual relations with the utmost care. Unsurprisingly, though, the bulk of the burden fell on girls and women (21, 9):

And the daughter of any priest, if she profane herself by playing the whore, she profaneth her father: she shall be burnt with fire.

Laying Down the Law

Forty years seems a very long time for an entire nation to wander in the wilderness – especially

in so confined a corner of the Middle East. It's difficult to avoid the suspicion that this section of the Bible is less about the literal itinerary

> 'if she profane herself by playing the whore, she profaneth her father.'
> LEVITICUS 21, 9

of the Jews with Moses and more about their moral and spiritual reconstruction as a people; a preparation for their life in the 'Promised Land'. This would explain the preoccupation of this part of the Bible – from Exodus, through Leviticus and on into the Book of Numbers – with the laying down of law and the establishment of custom.

The concept of 'cleanness' was central to the Jewish way of thinking at this time. It could be both physical and spiritual, and could be compromised in all sorts of different ways. One of these was by rebellion, the refusal to accept the authority of the appointed leadership. Hence the blighting of Miriam – Moses' own sister – when, in Numbers 12, 1, she and Aaron 'spake against Moses' asking 'Hath the Lord indeed spoken only by Moses? hath he not spoken also by us?' In punishment for this boldness of speech, we're told, Miriam (although not, significantly, her male co-critic Aaron) 'became leprous, white as snow' (12, 10). She was then 'shut out from the camp seven days', a temporary outcast, the better to come to understand her place. Further punishments are meted out for protests against

Opposite: The serpent-staff makes another appearance and works another miracle. This time (Numbers 21), appropriately enough, the brazen snake cures Israelites suffering from snakebites. Here we see them writhing in their pain.

Moses' leadership a little later (16, 31), when the ground opens up and swallows one unruly congregation: 'They went down alive into the pit, and the earth closed over them,' we are told. Shortly after, at 16, 49, illness is once again the scourge of God, and we find 14,700 wayward Jews being carried off by plague. And then again, when their unending wanderings in the wilderness was stirring up dissent (at 21, 6), 'the Lord sent fiery serpents among the people' – many, it is reported, died. Another 250 dissenters were swallowed up by the earth soon after (26, 13). God didn't take disobediences lightly, it appears.

MOSES AND THE MIDIANITES

'THOU SHALT NOT kill,' said the commandment – but, it seems, the Lord God himself was no fundamentalist. Murder in defence of his laws was not just accepted but acclaimed. Hence the praise for Phinehas, son of High Priest Eleazar. Hearing that a fellow Jew was consorting with a (pagan) Midianite woman, he 'took a javelin in his hand' (25, 7) and 'went after the man of Israel into the tent, and thrust both of them through, the man of Israel, and the woman through the belly.' This worthy deed, we're told (25, 8), didn't just cut short an awful miscegenation but also protected the children of Israel from the ravages of a plague that had already taken 24,000 lives.

The Midianites (the people to whom, we should not forget, Moses' father-in-law Jethro belonged) were to prove an uncomfortable thorn in Israel's side. When distrust finally flared up into open war, Moses was uncompromising in his language, urging his troops to 'kill every male among the little ones, and kill every woman that hath known man by lying with him' (31, 17). The virgin girls, however, were to be spared, and brought back amid the plunder: 32,000 of these prisoners were brought home.

The Conquest of Canaan

After 40 years in the desert, Moses finally died within sight of the Promised Land – although (Deuteronomy 34, 7) 'his eye was not dim, nor his natural force abated'. The succession as chief of the Israelite tribes passed to 'Joshua the son of Nun' since he was 'full of the spirit of wisdom' (34, 9) and the late patriarch had 'laid his hands upon him'. It was to Joshua that God now spoke (Joshua 1, 2), saying:

Now therefore arise, go over this Jordan, thou, and all this people, unto the land which I do give to them, even to the children of Israel … From the wilderness and this Lebanon even unto the great river, the river Euphrates, all the land of the Hittites, and unto the great sea toward the going down of the sun, shall be your coast.

Opposite: Moses scrambles to a mountain-top and – after 40 years' wandering with his people in the desert – is granted his first sight of the Promised Land. Ironically, it is also to be his last. His work now done, he dies.

The land may have been promised to the Jews, but that didn't mean they wouldn't have to exert themselves to get it. Most of it was already occupied by people who were not going to yield it meekly.

Directly in their way stood the city of Jericho – which was important strategically and, for Joshua's new leadership, symbolically. The story of the city's siege and capture is celebrated: for six days Joshua marched his army round its walls, his priests blasting away on their sacred ramshorn trumpets all the while. For six days the city walls stood firm, the garrison untroubled – increasingly derisive, indeed – but on the seventh day, as the trumpets sounded, they collapsed. 'Shout,' cried Joshua to his troops, 'for the Lord hath given you the city' (6, 16):

And they utterly destroyed all that was in the city, both man and woman, young and old, and ox, and sheep, and ass, with the edge of the sword. Jericho was now a Jewish city.

Storms of Slaughter

Ai, Gilgal, Gibeon, Makkedah, Libnah … the rest of the Book of Joshua goes by in a veritable catalogue of killing. During the capture of the city of Ai, 12,000 men and women were 'utterly destroyed' (8, 26) in a single day. The swords of Israel at Beth-horon were backed by 'great stones from heaven' (10, 11) – a destructive hailstorm sent by God himself to ensure that victory that day went to his Chosen People.

Having taken Hazor (11, 11), 'they smote all the souls that were therein with the edge of the sword, utterly destroying them: there was not any left to breathe: and he burnt Hazor with fire.' This is the rhetoric of genocide, of a people clearing a land of its inhabitants to make space for themselves. If it weren't also the rhetoric of epic exaggeration, it would be seriously damning.

Right: Joshua and his troops look on from a distance as the city of Ai goes up in flames. The Book of Jericho doesn't flinch from describing the carnage of the Canaan campaign: the Promised Land was to be won by force of arms.

THE HOLY HARLOT

As HE WORKED on his plans to capture Jericho, Joshua sent two of his men as spies to the city. They found a secret lodging in the home of the harlot Rahab (2, 1). Not only did Rahab take them in, but she bravely covered for them when men came to hunt them out, hiding them on her roof concealed beneath 'stalks of flax' (2, 6).

Rahab had, she said, heard the stories of the Jews, their deliverance from Egypt and the protection they'd received from the Lord their God. She helped them now in return for the protection of herself and her family. Then (2, 14):

she let them down by a cord through the window: for her house was upon the town wall, and she dwelt upon the wall.

So, with her help, the spies got clean away.

Later, when the town was taken, Joshua remembered Rahab's loyalty and courage. 'Only Rahab the harlot shall live,' he said (6, 17): 'she and all that are with her in her house.'

Right: Rahab's assistance to his spies was not to be forgotten by Joshua once he'd taken Jericho. She and her family were spared in the days that followed, when all the other people in the city were put to the sword.

'THOU SHALT SMITE THEM, AND UTTERLY DESTROY THEM'

The Jewish people consolidated their hold on Canaan in a campaign of cruel slaughter until the entire country had been bloodily subdued.

◆

'Ye have not obeyed my voice.'
JUDGES 2, 11.

The death of Joshua, at 110 years of age, left the Jewish nation leaderless – and, as believers, vulnerable to whatever more obviously enticing spirituality came their way. The period that followed saw frequent backsliding into paganism – often God or

Opposite: A hero in harness: Samson, shorn of his strength-giving locks, is forced to drive a mill for the Philistines. Carl Bloch's 1863 painting points up its subject's beauty at the expense of showing that he has been blinded in both eyes.

Yahweh was rejected in favour of other cults; sometimes that of the ancient Semitic deity known as Baal. 'I the Lord thy God am a jealous God,' Yahweh had reminded Moses as he gave him his Commandments (Exodus 20, 5): he certainly didn't take kindly to the adoration of rivals now. 'And the anger of the Lord was hot against Israel,' we read, 'and he delivered them into the hands of spoilers that spoiled them, and he sold them into the hands of their enemies round about.'

'Evil in the Sight of the Lord'

Despite this, we are told, 'the Lord raised up judges, which delivered them out of the hand

of those that spoiled them.' This book of the Bible is actually known as the Book of Judges – the title does not seem to imply any sort of legal background: just tribal leadership, and the backing of the Lord. These men were 'judges' in that they imposed and administered the law on God's behalf. Even so, they could not necessarily command the loyalty or obedience of their people. For, it is reported (Judges 2, 17), the Jews:

would not hearken unto their judges, but they went a whoring after other gods, and bowed themselves unto them: they turned quickly out of the way which their fathers walked in.

This backsliding into paganism was to be a feature of the time. It is signalled by formulations like 'And the children of Israel did evil in the sight of the Lord' – at chapter 2, verse 11. Much the same report is made in close-to-identical words at 3, 12; 4, 1; and 6, 1, for example. Each time, fortunately for the Jews, a new Judge took charge and led his people back on to the monotheistic 'way ... their fathers walked in'.

Typically, they imposed their authority, not by their learning, their eloquence or their stoic dignity but by their military prowess – like that of Shamgar, 'which slew of the Philistines six hundred men with an ox goad' (3, 31).

Moabite Massacre

One longstanding conflict in Canaan was with the Moabites, a pagan people occupying the area to the east of the Dead Sea. The children of Israel once again doing 'evil in the sight of the Lord', God grew angry and 'strengthened Eglon the king of Moab against Israel' (3, 12).

With his allies from the lands of Ammon and Amalek, he 'smote' Israel and took its children under domination.

The Jews were crying out to the Lord in penitence, and he 'raised them up a deliverer' (3, 15) in the person of Ehud, son of Gera, 'a man lefthanded'. He was sent as an emissary

to take a gift to Eglon, King of Moab. But, the Book of Judges tells us:

Ehud made him a dagger which had two edges … and he did gird it under his raiment upon his right thigh. And he brought the present unto Eglon king of Moab; and Eglon was a very fat man … And Ehud said, I have a message from God unto thee. And he arose out of his seat. And Ehud put forth his left hand, and took the dagger from his right thigh, and thrust it into his belly: And the haft also went in after the blade; and the fat closed upon the blade, so that he could not draw the dagger out of his belly; and the dirt came out.

Emboldened by his actions, his fellow Jews attacked the Moabites (3, 29):

And they slew of Moab at that time about ten thousand men, all lusty, and all men of valour; and there escaped not a man.

A Woman's Place

Jewish society at this time was for the most part, quite literally, a 'patriarchy', but this didn't necessarily mean that women didn't play an important role. And not just as wives

---

'And the fat closed upon the blade, so that he could not draw the dagger out of his belly'.

JUDGES 3, 22

---

and mothers: Deborah, wife of Lapidoth, for instance, was revered as a 'prophetess' (4, 4). More than this, we're told: 'she judged Israel at that time' – she was, in short, a leader of her nation.

This said, Deborah's authority doesn't seem to have been sufficient to dissuade the Jews from one of their periodic swings back into paganism. God, in his anger, had 'sold them into the hand of Jabin king of Canaan, that reigned in Hazor' (4, 3). Jabin was, by any ancient standards, an impressively powerful overlord: 'for he had nine hundred chariots of iron; and twenty years he mightily oppressed the children of Israel' (4, 3).

Deborah was determined to save her people, though. Calling upon Barak, son of Abinoam, she ordered him to take an army 10,000 strong towards Mount Tabor, where he might attack King Jabin's army under its feared commander, Sisera. An apprehensive Barak replied 'If thou wilt go with me, then I will go; but if thou wilt not go with me, then I will not go.' Deborah promised her support, while warning him that the glory of the campaign would not ultimately

Left: Eglon, King of the Moabites, falls dead, brought down by the dagger which Ehud has been carrying concealed on his thigh beneath his clothing. This, it seems, was the 'message from God' which the Jewish Judge had brought.

come to him, 'for the Lord shall sell Sisera into the hand of a woman' (4, 9).

This was a little unfair, perhaps, for Barak and his army did get their victory in the field of battle (4, 15):

The Lord discomfited Sisera, and all his chariots, and all his host, with the edge of the sword before Barak.

Sisera, in his panic, jumped down from his chariot 'and fled away quickly on his feet', with Barak and his host in hot pursuit. But they could not catch Jabin's captain, who took refuge in the tent of his friend and also his ally Heber the Kenite.

But Heber's wife Jael was not quite so sympathetic. She felt for the Jews, who had so long suffered at Sisera and Jabin's hands. Even so, she stepped forward to welcome the fugitive, the perfect hostess. Ushering him into her husband's tent, she persuaded him to lie down and rest in his weariness. She even covered him with a mantle for his comfort:

Above: Deborah, wife of Lapidoth, was held in reverence as a prophet. The first (and only) female Judge, she led the Jews in rebellion against Canaan's oppressive King Jabin, gaining victory with the help of another woman, Jael.

And he said unto her, Give me, I pray thee, a little water to drink; for I am thirsty. And she opened a bottle of milk, and gave him drink, and covered him. Again he said unto her, Stand in the door of the tent, and it shall be, when any man doth come and enquire of thee, and say, Is there any man here? that thou shalt say, No. (4, 19)

So it was agreed, and so Sisera turned in to rest, reassured of his safety.

Then, however (4, 21):

Jael Heber's wife took a nail of the tent, and took an hammer in her hand, and went softly unto him, and smote the nail into his temples, and fastened it into the ground: for he was fast asleep and weary. So he died.

When Barak arrived in pursuit of Sisera, Jael welcomed him in his turn, saying 'Come, and I will shew thee the man whom thou seekest' (4, 22):

And when he came into her tent, behold, Sisera lay dead, and the nail was in his temples.

Left: Jael displays her trophy to Barak, Deborah's general. Having welcomed Sisera, made the enemy commander as comfortable as any conscientious hostess should, she had driven an iron spike through his head as he lay in slumber.

to secure the succession for himself. That he was 71st in line to the title of Judge does not seem to have deterred him. With the help of his mother's family, he murdered them – bashing out the brains of 69 'upon one stone' (9, 5). Only the youngest, Jotham, managed to slip away and hide.

Jotham cursed Abimelech and his house and his reign as Judge. He enlisted the help of a neighbouring ruler, Gaal, in a war with Abimelech's Israel – without success, though, for Abimelech won the day.

Abimelech seemed invincible in battle. Ironically, it was to take a woman to overthrow him as well. Laying siege to the city of Thabaz, he breached its defences and was attacking the central tower in which the garrison and their families had holed up when he was hit on the head by a 'piece of millstone', hurled from a high battlement by a woman trapped inside (9, 53). Seeing that he was being brought to his death by a female attacker, and unwilling to endure the ignominy, he called on his armour-bearer to 'thrust him through' (9, 54).

Just as Deborah had prophesied, then, Jabin and Sisera had been defeated by the men of Israel, but the honour of the victory rested with a woman.

The Bastard and his Brothers

Barak succeeded Deborah as Judge, to be followed in his turn by Gideon – chiefly remarkable, perhaps, in having 'threescore and ten' – or seventy – sons. Threescore and eleven in actual fact, for he sired another boy with a concubine. Abimelech (the name means 'my father, king', so can be seen as a defiantly asserting a right to rule) grew up determined

Opposite: Slain by a stone hurled from the battlements above by a woman of the city, Abimelech lies dead outside the walls of Thabaz. He had his swordbearer run him through to spare him the shame of being killed by a woman.

A HIGH PRICE

GOD SHOWED HIS impatience with his people when – once again angered at Israel's return to dabbling in pagan practices – he gave them over to the domination of the Ammonites. He was to prove exacting in the amends he demanded from the Jews. Anxious to secure his people's freedom, Judge Jephthah 'vowed a vow unto the Lord' (11, 30), promising that, if he would assure Israel victory:

Then it shall be that, whatsoever cometh forth of the doors of my house to meet me, when I return in peace from the children of Ammon, shall surely be the Lord's, and I will offer it up for a burnt offering.

God gave him his victory but, returning home in triumph, Jephthah found his jubilation turning to despair when his beloved daughter came rushing out of the house to meet him.

A model for Jewish girlhood, Jephthah's (unnamed) daughter, accepted her grisly destiny without repining. She asked only for two months' grace, 'that I might go up and down upon the mountains, and bewail my virginity' (11, 37).

A Hairy Hero

And so the cycle continued: in adversity, the Jews remembered their God; as soon as he restored prosperity, they invariably wavered in their faith. God, angered as he was by their apostasy, always came to his people's rescue, providing some leader or hero who could help them.

One of these was Samson. He was born to a man named Manoah and his wife, who were unable to have children: the angel who brought Manoah's wife the good news warned her that God insisted, as a condition of allowing her to conceive, that no razor should ever touch the head of the son she bore (13, 5).

Samson grew up a hero of a fairly straightforward sort – albeit wayward from the first in his romantic aspirations. Despite his parents' disapproval, he set his sights on a beautiful young woman of the Philistine people

Left: Jephthah's obedience unto death – and her valuing of her virginity above her life – made her a model for feminine propriety well into modern times. Painted around 1660, the maiden's fate, though lamented, is never for a moment questioned.

– pagans and enemies of the Jews. On his way to see her one day, he was attacked by a lion but was able to pull it physically apart with the incredible strength of his hands.

Sweetness, Strength and Savagery

A standard superhero story, then. Later, though, the plot was to thicken. Passing by the same place, Samson saw that there was a nest of bees, full of honey, inside the lion's carcass.

Samson used this as the basis for a riddle to confound his fiancée's family's Philistine acquaintances. If they could solve it, he said, he would give them 'thirty sheets and thirty changes of garments' (14, 12). 'Out of the eater came forth meat,' went the riddle; 'and out of the strong came forth sweetness' (14, 14). The 'meat' here (in its old sense, of meaning simply 'food') was the honey, which had come out of the lion's belly; the sweetness too was the honey from inside the 'strong', the lion.

Driven almost demented by their inability to solve this riddle, the Philistines threatened to kill his bride if she didn't reveal the answer: when

she did, it was Samson who was mad with rage. Immediately embarking on his own one-man war with the Philistines, he killed 30 of their young men at random and took the clothes off their backs to settle up his wager (14, 19).

Not surprisingly, his father-in-law reconsidered and gave his wife to another in marriage. 'I verily thought that thou hadst utterly hated her,' he insisted (15, 2). (More remarkably, he said that Samson could still wed her younger sister.) Samson erupted into a fury all over again and, since the wheat harvest was fast approaching, he:

went and caught three hundred foxes, and took firebrands, and turned tail to tail, and put a firebrand in the midst between two tails. And when he had set the brands on fire, he let them go into the standing corn of the Philistines.

In revenge for this, the Philistines burned

Above: Schooled in the classical learning of the Renaissance, artists found themselves irresistibly drawn to see Jewish Samson as a version of the Greek strongman Hercules. He too had wrestled with a lion, as the biblical hero does here.

both his sometime bride and her father to death. And in revenge for *that*, Samson 'smote' the Philistines 'hip and thigh with a great slaughter' (15, 8).

When a Philistine army marched down to confront the Jews, demanding that Samson be given up to them, safely bound up in cords, Samson told his comrades that they should tie him and hand him over as required – he would happily comply. Once he was behind the Philistine lines, however (15, 14):

the Spirit of the Lord came mightily upon him, and the cords that were upon his arms became as flax that was burnt with fire, and his bands loosed from off his hands. And he found a new jawbone of an ass, and put forth his hand, and took it, and slew a thousand men therewith.

Deadly Delilah

The story of Samson and Delilah is the archetypal tale of the strong, straightforward man brought to his destruction by the wiles of womanhood. Delilah was approached by the Philistines as soon as Samson's interest in her became known: 'Entice him, and see wherein his great strength lieth,' they urged her (16, 5).

Delilah duly asked him and – apparently amused – he told her that his strength would ebb away if he were bound with bowstrings. The Philistines tried that while he slept – but when he woke, he broke them. Urged again, he said that his strength might be thwarted if he were tied up with fresh-made ropes: these were tried, and these too proved unavailing.

Delilah pressed and, finally, he confided that the loss of his hair would drain him of all his strength: he described the prohibition the angel had issued before his birth. And so (16, 19):

she made him sleep upon her knees; and she called for a man, and she caused him to shave off the seven locks of his head; and she began to afflict him, and his strength went from him.

As if this symbolic castration weren't enough, the Philistines promptly performed a second one, putting out his eyes – just as Sophocles' King Oedipus did, tormented by the guilt of his incestuous relations with his mother.

Right: Towering above the mass of enemy troops, brandishing an ass's jawbone about his head, Samson sets about the smiting of the Philistines. This dramatic engraving was created by Gustave Doré in the nineteenth century.

> ' ... she caused him to shave off the seven locks of his head; and she began to afflict him...'
>
> JUDGES 16, 19

Brought down by his beloved's treachery, Samson was at his lowest, utterly abased: planning to parade him at one of their feasts, the Philistines pulled him from his prison. 'Now the house was full of men and women,' we're told (16, 27):

and all the lords of the Philistines were there; and there were upon the roof about three thousand men and women, that beheld while Samson made sport.

But Samson called on God for help (16, 28):

O Lord God, remember me, I pray thee, and strengthen me, I pray thee, only this once, O God, that I may be at once avenged of the Philistines for my two eyes. And Samson took hold of the two middle pillars upon which the house stood, and on which it was borne up, of the one with his right hand, and of the other with his left. And Samson said, Let me die with the Philistines. And he bowed himself with all his might; and the house fell upon the lords, and upon all the people that were therein.

Beating the Benjamites

The smiting continued, now with civil war between the Tribe of Benjamin (descendants of Joseph's younger brother) and the rest of Israel. The Benjamites refused to respect the 'voice of their brethren' (20, 13) in the other tribes. Hostilities opened with an attack by the children of Benjamin that, according to Judges (20, 21), 'destroyed down to the ground of the Israelites … twenty and two thousand men'. A few days later, 'Benjamin went forth' a second time 'and destroyed down to the ground of the children of Israel again eighteen thousand men' (20, 25). Although far superior in numbers, the other tribes were at first caught unprepared: the Benjamites seemed to be able to bully them at will. Soon, though, the tables were turned, and at a major engagement outside the city of Gibeah (20, 36):

the Lord smote Benjamin before Israel; and the children of Israel destroyed of the Benjamites that day twenty and five thousand and an hundred men.

Their city in flames, they fled for the wilderness, but 'the battle overtook them' (20, 42) and a further 'eighteen thousand' Benjamite lives were claimed.

Left: Jan Lievens' 1635 Delilah is not the delicate and subtle seductress the nineteenth-century decadents loved to fantasize about but an aggressive thug-in-female-form. It is clear from the painting that this woman inspires fear even in the Philistines.

HOSTLY DUTY

An episode in Chapter 19 of the Book of Judges brings us biblical morality at its most perplexing. In some ways reminiscent of the story of Sodom, it shows the masculine code of hospitality trumping just about everything else. Even, it seems, the need to protect women from gang rape.

The story relates how an old man in the town of Gibeah took a weary wayfarer, travelling with his 'handmaiden' or 'concubine' into his home. 'So he brought him into his house … and they washed their feet and did eat and drink' (19, 21).

As the evening wore on, however, and the old man's company 'were making their hearts merry' (19, 22):

the men of the city … beset the house round about, and beat at the door, and spake to the master of the house, the old man, saying, Bring forth the man that came into thine house, that we may know him.

The householder emerged and tried to reason with this rapacious mob: 'I pray you, do not so wickedly; seeing that this man is come into mine house, do not this folly.' Seeing them still implacable, he offered them a compromise (19, 24):

Behold, here is my daughter a maiden, and his concubine; them I will bring out now, and humble ye them, and do with them what seemeth good unto you; but unto this man do not so vile a thing.

But the men were not to be dissuaded and carried on clamouring for the male guest to be given up to their lust. At this point, in desperation, the traveller brought his concubine out and handed her over to the baying crowd. 'And they knew her, and abused her all the

Above: 'The Levite Findeth his Dead Wife'. Horrified and fascinated by the connection they sensed between eroticism and violence, nineteenth-century artists were repeatedly drawn to the strange sexual politics of the Old Testament.

night until the morning; and when the day began to spring, they let her go.' Then, the account continues (19, 26):

came the woman in the dawning of the day, and fell down at the door of the man's house where her lord was, till it was light.

There her master found her when he awoke – she, alas, was not to be awoken. Carrying her body into the house, he cut her up ('together with her bones' – 19, 29), and sent the pieces 'into all the coasts of Israel'. So outraged were the Jews at the men of Gibeah's outrageous breach of hospitality (20, 11) that 'all the men of Israel were gathered against the city, knit together as one man'.

Above: The Israelites could be their own worst enemies – quite literally, when it came to the war between the Benjamites and the other tribes, a civil conflict which put most of the Jews' external wars in the shade.

Allowable Abduction

By now the Tribe of Benjamin had been all but extinguished, but the enmity still continued – so much so that the other tribes agreed not to give the Benjamites their daughters in marriage. At the same time, it did not sit comfortably with them that a tribe of Israel should simply die out (21, 15): 'And the people repented them for Benjamin, because that the Lord had made a breach in the tribes of Israel.' Then, we're told, the elders asked:

How shall we do for wives for them that remain, seeing the women are destroyed out of Benjamin? ... Howbeit we may not give them wives of our daughters; for the children of Israel

have sworn, saying, Cursed be he that giveth a wife to Benjamin.'

The answer was to sanction large-scale rape: the elders urged the Benjamites to lie in wait by the vineyards of Shiloh, north of Bethel, and abduct the daughters of the city as they danced at their annual festivities.

An Intimate Revenge

It was Israel's turn to suffer massacre when hostilities with the Philistines were renewed, as depicted in the First Book of Samuel. In scenes of 'very great slaughter', 30,000 Israelites were slain (4, 10), and the sacred Ark of the Covenant was seized and taken to the city of Ashdod.

Right: The sons of Benjamin carry off the daughters of Shiloh – compelled to do so, they claimed, by the refusal of the other tribes to grant them wives. The story echoes the Roman myth of the Rape of the Sabine Women.

God exacted vengeance on his people's behalf soon after, though: he took the capture of the Ark as an unpardonable affront. The Philistines bore their trophy back in triumph to the temple of their idol, Dagon. Next morning, they found that the figure of their deity had toppled over in the night and was lying flat on its face on the temple floor (5, 3).

And this was just the start. 'The hand of the Lord was against the city with a very great destruction', we're told (5, 9):

and he smote the men of the city, both small and great, and they had emerods in their secret parts.

In fear, the Philistines moved the Ark – first to the city of Gath, and then after that to Ekron

Below: A talisman taken. The Israelites carry their Ark of Covenant into battle, believing it will bring them guaranteed glory. Instead, it is captured by the Philistines, who inflict ignominious defeat – and 'very great slaughter' on the Jews.

Above: Buckled over in their pain – and their indignity – the men of Ashdod have cause to rue their recent triumph. The 'emerods in their secret parts' have been sent by God in punishment for their capture of the Ark of Covenant.

– but in those places too people were subjected to the painful and undignified affliction of emerods (haemorrhoids).

In despair, the Philistines turned to their 'priests and diviners' for advice. They told them that they would have to return the Ark of the Covenant to the Jews. In addition, they said, the Philistines would have to make a 'trespass offering' (6, 9) to atone for their crime: five golden 'emerods', and five golden mice – one for each of the five chiefs of the Philistines.

And so the Ark of the Covenant, carried in state on a specially constructed cart drawn by a pair of 'milch cows', set out on its journey back to Israelite territory. But the smiting on its account was not yet done. On its final stop, at the city of Beth-shemesh, local men opened the lid of the Ark and peered in. God was enraged at this act of sacrilege (6, 19):

and he smote the men of the Beth-shemesh, because they had looked into the ark of the Lord, even he smote of the people fifty thousand and threescore and ten men.

The Coming of the Kings

It was at about this time that Samuel came to the fore: the last of Israel's Judges, he was at the same time the first of those divinely-inspired seers and preachers known as prophets. Their lives and teachings were to be the focus of the Bible in its next few books. Samuel was significant too, however, in ushering in the age of kings – those royal rulers who would bring

> '... ye shall cry out in that day because of your king which ye shall have chosen you'.
>
> SAMUEL 8, 18

what had been a loose tribal federation together into a single Jewish state.

Samuel had built a personal reputation for himself by leading his people in successful expeditions against the Philistines, the Ammonites and the Amalekites. As he approached his death (8, 5), the people asked him to appoint a king. Although this request 'displeased' him, he prayed to God for guidance: the Lord instructed him to tell the Jews that they could have a king, but that he would tax and tyrannize them beyond all endurance. And (8, 18):

ye shall cry out in that day because of your king which ye shall have chosen you; and the Lord will not hear you in that day.

Even so, the people insisted, so Samuel anointed Saul first King of Israel: he led the Jews to victory over the Moabites, the Ammonites and Edomites, as well as other foes. But his sons – and likely successors – were dishonest, and Saul himself avaricious. Things came to a head when he defeated the Amalekites (15, 7): the Lord had commanded him to destroy the whole people and all they had. When the moment came, however, Saul took it upon himself to spare their king, Agag, and the best of their livestock. God would never forgive this disobedience.

'An evil spirit from the Lord' was to make Saul's life wretched from this time on. The

Above: Racked by 'emerods', brought low by pain, the Philistines feel they have no alternative but to return to its rightful owners the Ark which they bore back to Ashdod so recently and in such great triumph.

only thing that could calm him was one of his younger servants who was 'a cunning player on an harp' (16, 16). David, son of Jesse, a shepherd boy tending his father's flocks when he wasn't helping to carry King Saul's weapons for him or entertaining him with his songs, was in time to play a far more important role.

David and Goliath

It was in mountainous country outside the city of Shochoh in Judah that the Jews and the Philistines next came to confrontation. Israel's forces were shocked to see the Philistine champion take to the field. Goliath of Gath stood 'six cubits and a span' (so almost ten feet or three metres) tall:

And he had an helmet of brass upon his head, and he was armed with a coat of mail; and the weight of the coat was five thousand shekels of brass … And the staff of his spear was like a weavers' beam; and his spear's head weighed six hundred shekels of iron (17, 5).

This giant mocked the Israelites, challenging them to find a champion who might be able to match him. None would step forward, for (unsurprisingly) 'they were dismayed, and greatly afraid' (17, 11).

Only David would go out to meet Goliath. With some misgivings, Saul agreed to let him: he tried to arm him, but David preferred to use weapons of his own (17, 40):

And he took his staff in his hand, and chose him five smooth stones out of the brook, and put them in a shepherd's bag which he had … and his sling was in his hand.

Seeing this mere boy approach him, Goliath 'disdained' him and asked 'Am I a dog, that thou comest to me with staves?' But as Goliath came at him, his spear raised, David (17, 49):

put his hand in his bag, and took thence a stone, and slang it, and smote the Philistine in his forehead, that the stone sunk into his forehead; and he fell upon his face to the earth.

Below: David delights Saul with his playing – so much so that the 'evil spirit' is driven out from him. David's harp was the only thing that could calm the King, and the shepherd-boy became his close attendant.

Left: David stands over his fallen foe, holding up his severed head as a grisly trophy. In the background, the Philistines flee whilst the Israelites give thanks. The famous scene is here depicted by De Sayvede Oude (1624).

Running forward, he seized his enemy's own sword, 'and drew it out of the sheath thereof, and slew him, and cut off his head therewith' (17, 51). Seeing their champion slain, the Philistines fled.

A King Eclipsed

And this was just the start. From now on (18, 5), David:

went out whithersoever Saul sent him, and behaved himself wisely; and Saul set him over the men of war, and he was accepted in the sight of all the people … And it came to pass as they came, when David was returned from the slaughter of the Philistine, that the women came out of all cities of Israel, singing and dancing, to meet king Saul, with tabrets, with joy, and with instruments of musick.

Like the 'timbrel' played upon by Miriam (see previous chapter, 'Way Across the Water' section), the 'tabret' was a small hand-drum. Suffice it to say that David's triumphs were very noisily acclaimed. More so than his master's perhaps (18, 7):

And the women answered one another as they played, and said, Saul hath slain his thousands, and David his ten thousands.

Suffering such comparisons, Saul was 'wroth'. Where would this adulation end? Where could it, but in his own displacement on the throne? 'The evil spirit from God came upon Saul' once more (18, 10):

and David played with his hand, as at other times; and there was a javelin in Saul's hand. And Saul cast the javelin; for he said, I will smite David even to the wall with it. And David avoided out of his presence twice.

In calmer frame of mind, the King was able to think more cunningly. He married David to his daughter Michal, to bind him closer. But each fresh triumph of his son-in-law's was a new humiliation: his murderous rage towards David only grew. At last, after another javelin attack, Michal – who truly loved her husband – grew so fearful for his safety that she told him to escape. 'If thou save not thy life to night,' she said (19, 11), 'to morrow thou shalt be slain.'

Below: The 'evil spirit from the Lord' never left King Saul, though the torments in his mind might temporarily be soothed by David's playing. More than once, he attacked his beloved minstrel with a javelin.

'NO SUCH THING OUGHT TO BE DONE IN ISRAEL'

The Kingdom of Israel now established, there was leisure for more civilized sins – seductions, betrayals, infidelities and intrigues. But the battlefield slaughters continued as before.

'The adversaries of the Lord shall be broken to pieces.' 1 SAMUEL 2, 10.

David is a pivotal figure in many ways. Saul's successor succeeded (as Saul hadn't really managed) in bringing Israel's tribes together into something like a nation as we would nowadays understand it. Later, for Christians, his reign would provide a sort of spiritual template for their Saviour's. (Jesus' father, Joseph, of course, claimed descent from the great king.) It's arguable too that

Opposite: In Philip R. Morris' nineteenth-century painting, Jonathan rehearses the signal by which he will let David (who's leaving Saul's service) know if it's safe to return to visit him or if he needs to stay away.

David, as the composer of the Psalms, was one of the first great poets of all time, who brought a new lyricism – a more intimate, personal feel, perhaps – to a Bible narrative that had come to be dominated by stories of battle and slaughter. The first obvious example of this is that of the love that sprang up between David and Saul's son Jonathan – a love that is as obviously deep as it is undefined.

'Passing the Love of Women'

In the Bible narrative, the epic and the lyric strands were very closely intertwined. The two youths met in the first flush of David's victory over Goliath. Jonathan was with his father when the shepherd boy came back to report to Saul (1 Samuel 18, 1):

And it came to pass, when he had made an end

of speaking unto Saul, that the soul of Jonathan was knit with the soul of David, and Jonathan loved him as his own soul.

Jonathan's love for his hero was advanced by his father's admiration for his protégé, for Saul took David into his own house and would not let him go back to his father's (18, 2):

Then Jonathan and David made a covenant, because he loved him as his own soul. And Jonathan stripped himself of the robe that was upon him, and gave it to David, and his garments, even to his sword, and to his girdle.

If this little scene of Jonathan's undressing carries an erotic charge, it's never earthed

in anything more explicit. Were David and Jonathan 'gay' lovers, as we would understand it? The biblical account is coy – or unconcerned. But the high-minded view that it doesn't matter either way has never been good enough for those traditional moralists who are outraged at the very suggestion of a sexual relationship between the two men. Or – more recently – for those who would see them as gay-rights pioneers.

Whatever the nature of their relationship, it was evidently extremely close and deep. When Jonathan was killed in battle on Mount Gilboa, and his father, Saul, committed suicide in his own grief, the inconsolable David mourned both men's death in a heartrending lament (2 Samuel 1, 19):

The beauty of Israel is slain upon thy high places: how are the mighty fallen! ...Ye mountains of Gilboa, let there be no dew, neither let there be rain, upon you, nor fields of offerings.

For Jonathan there was special praise: if David's tribute 'very pleasant hast thou been unto me' (1, 26) sounds underwhelming to modern ears, it's rounded off with a more obviously impassioned tribute: 'thy love to me was wonderful, passing the love of women.'

Displeasing to the Lord

Not that David was one to turn up his nose at the 'love of women'. One sleepless

Left: David bows before Jonathan in token of the respect which is due to him as the King his master's son: then, however, with greater intimacy, 'they kissed one another, and wept with one another' (1 Samuel 20, 41).

evening, indeed, going up on to his palace roof in Jerusalem to take the air, 'from the roof he saw a woman washing herself; and the woman was very beautiful to look upon' (2 Samuel 11, 2). The king sent for the woman: her name was Bathsheba, and she was married to a man named Uriah. Despite this David made her his mistress. Soon he had word from her that she had conceived and was 'with child' (11, 5), at which point a romantic story of forbidden love (or a squalid case of sexual exploitation, depending on how one looks at it), became something more serious and sinister.

Bathsheba's pregnancy was not just an inconvenience and a moral shame but, potentially, a political scandal. Uriah was away, doing his patriotic duty fighting the Ammonites at the siege of Rabbah, while David was at home consorting with his wife. Concerned to cover his

Above: With an incongruously courteous tip of the hat, King David's messenger in this sixteenth-century engraving accosts the bathing Bathsheba, bringing her the royal summons from his master. The young wife seems completely unperturbed.

tracks, the king had Uriah summoned back to Jerusalem to report on the progress of the war. Having heard what he had to say, he sent him home to relax – and, he clearly hoped, to have sexual relations with his wife. But Uriah, loyal to his comrades 'encamped in the open fields' (11, 11) and exposed to all the risks of war, didn't consider this appropriate: 'Shall I then go into mine house, to eat and to drink, and to lie with my wife?'

What had seemed a cunning plan thwarted, the king in his frustration wrote a secret letter to Uriah's general, Joab. 'Set ye Uriah in the forefront of the hottest battle,' the letter read, 'and retire ye from him, that he may be smitten, and die' (11, 15). So, when the unwitting Uriah returned to the front he carried with him his own death warrant. This time, David's strategy was successful. The story had a happy ending of sorts: having mourned her husband for the

> 'Having mourned her husband for the appointed time, Bathsheba married her lord and lover'.

appointed time, Bathsheba married her lord and lover. 'But the thing that David had done displeased the Lord' (11, 27). Bathsheba bore a baby son, but he soon fell sick. For all David's fasting and prayers of repentance, the boy died (12, 18).

All in the Family

David's first wife, we saw in the last section of the previous chapter, was Michal, the daughter of Saul. Bathsheba, widow of Uriah, was number eight. The others flit by all but unnoticed in the Bible narrative, as for the most part do the miscellaneous concubines whose sons, however, are acknowledged later in the Books of Chronicles.

Since polygamy was, at this time, not just lawful for the Jews but an established custom, there's nothing intrinsically 'dark' about it, it might be said. But, like any system of family construction, it came accompanied by its own set of difficulties and tensions that could on occasion erupt into ferocious violence.

Right: Pikemen and armoured knights fill the foreground of what is a much larger, medieval painting representing the Siege of Rabat. King David sent Bathsheba's husband Uriah to the frontline here, knowing that it meant his certain death.

ISLAMIC DAVID

DAVID, BEING BOTH a prophet and a king, has a special significance for Muslims. In an Islamic tradition that has never accepted the modern Western idea of a separation of powers of religion and the state, he may even be seen as a prototype for the Muslim Caliph.

There is no place in the Islamic narrative for the flawed and fallible figure of Jewish and Christian tradition. The story of David and Bathsheba – and of the murder of Uriah – are absent here.

So it was with Amnon, son of David's second wife Ahinoam, who had married him after his flight from Saul – and, necessarily then, from Michal. As he grew into manhood, Amnon found himself falling in love with Tamar, David's daughter by Maachah, a younger queen. As half-siblings, the two could have no lawful sexual relations, but Amnon's desire kept growing and would not be suppressed.

Eventually, in utter despair and frustration, Amnon consulted his friend Jonadab ('a very subtil man', 13, 3). On his advice, he remained in his room one day, pretending to be ill. He

Below: Tamar brings food to her half-brother, under the impression that he's ill. In fact, it's a ruse so he can get her close to him and rape her. Having had his way, he hates her 'exceedingly', and drives her from his house.

AN OEDIPAL STRUGGLE

DAVID'S THIRD SON, Absalom, was the pride not only of his father but of his people. He wasn't merely handsome, he was perfect (14, 25):

In all Israel there was none to be so much praised as Absalom for his beauty: from the sole of his foot even to the crown of his head there was no blemish in him.

It seemed only natural that such a paragon of princes should have his own impressive retinue of 'chariots and horses' (15, 1), and 'fifty men to run before him' as he went.

It was perhaps inevitable too that Absalom should start envying his father's authority. Soon he was setting himself up as a rival to David, waiting by the gate of Jerusalem to ask visitors their business and hearing cases they had hoped to bring before the king. In this way, we are told, Absalom 'stole the hearts of the men of Israel' (15, 6) – David was being sidelined by his son.

Absalom's rivalry with his father was quite clearly the sort that Sigmund Freud was later to characterize as 'oedipal'. He named his complex, of course, after Oedipus, the character in Sophocles' play who killed his father, Laius, before marrying his mother, Jocasta.

Oedipus Tyrannus is of course a tragedy of errors: Oedipus has no idea who his father is when he kills him; nor do either he or his mother have the slightest awareness of their ensuing 'crime'. Freud might profitably have asked himself what subconscious force prompted him to look to the classical sources for prototypes of psychological tensions that were only too clearly evidenced in the scriptural traditions of his own Jewish background.

Absalom's resentment against his father

Above: Turning heads, of both sexes, Absalom steals the hearts of the Jewish people. But this adulation is not enough for King David's third son, who must outdo his father, or die (and kill – even massacre) in the attempt.

finally flared up into an out-and-out revolt against his royal rule – which began with the son's rape of his father's concubines. In all, 20,000 fell in the ensuing slaughter. Absalom himself was killed and his father devastated. The tensions of the father–son relationship were never so strikingly dramatized.

begged his father that his half-sister Tamar should come and tend him. She dutifully complied, bringing him some cakes to eat. But he 'took hold of her, and said unto her, Come lie with me, my sister' (13, 11). When she refused, Amnon, 'being stronger than she, forced her, and lay with her.'

As soon as he'd had his way, Amnon felt an overpowering sense of repulsion. He 'hated her exceedingly' (13, 15), 'so that the hatred wherewith he hated her was greater than the love wherewith he had loved her.' He drove her angrily from his house, 'And Tamar put ashes on her head, and rent her garment' (13, 19).

Two years later, her younger brother Absalom avenged her wrong. He hosted a feast, got Amnon drunk and had his servants assassinate him on his way home.

A Sinful Census

The early history of the Jews in Canaan saw a cycle of prosperity, paganism, punishment and penitence for a people whose loyalty to their one God was only gradually secured. Now, however, that Judaism had been firmly established in something like its final form, rival religions no longer appealed. There were still temptations, though: with all the rich trappings of regal power around him, the king was in danger of making an idolatry of his own self-regard. So, at least, seems to have been the case with David, and his desire to extend his own personal power as monarch through

Left: The Angel of Death descends over Israel bringing pestilence (in 2 Samuel 24), with the loss of 70,000 lives. The Lord had apparently been angered by David's presumption in conducting a census of his kingdom.

'With all the rich trappings of regal power around him, the king was in danger of making an idolatry of his own self-regard'.

the conducting of a census in 2 Samuel, Chapter 24. His intention appears to have been to ascertain the number of recruits he could call on for his armies – a judiciously far-sighted aim, perhaps, but one that set his own secular considerations as king above his duty to the Lord. Furious at what he saw as an act of insubordination, God sent down a 'pestilence' that took the lives of 70,000 people.

Wisdom – and Ruthlessness

Bathsheba's second, and surviving, son was to be David's heir. Solomon is primarily remembered for his wisdom. Most famously, he arbitrated (1 Kings, Chapter 3) between the two women who argued over who was the mother of an infant son by calling on one of his guards to cut the boy in half. (Both had just borne sons, but one had accidentally killed her child by overlaying him in bed.) While the fraudulent mother seized on Solomon's solution, her opponent showed her true maternal devotion

Below: Clever, or just callous? Solomon makes his famous 'Judgement' in the case of the two women claiming a single child. When he suggested cutting the boy in two, the real mother backed down. Depicted by Peter Paul Rubens (c. 1617).

by immediately relenting, and relinquishing her claim. A good story – although it does at the same time suggest a ruthless streak in Solomon, one that was to be manifested in other areas of his life.

Solomon's action in executing David's leading general, Joab, may have been the deathbed wish of his father, angered by his disloyalty, but it certainly suited him to have a potential threat removed. His elder brother Adonijah arguably had a better claim to the throne than he did, but Solomon showed no pity when he rebelled against his rule.

'Strange Women'

Solomon, we learn in the First Book of Kings (11, 3), had 'seven hundred wives, princesses, and three hundred concubines'. An impressive – even alarming – total to the modern reader, but the sheer number of royal bedmates doesn't bother the biblical narrator. What does is the fact that so many of the women whom

Right: Received in royal splendour, the Queen of Sheba with her retinue makes her obeisances before King Solomon. According to 1 Kings 10, she came to discuss theological questions, but it's the opulence of her visit which has been remembered ever since.

AN ENIGMATIC GUEST

OF ALL THE 'strange women' in Solomon's life, none has left more of a mark than the Queen of Sheba – although she is essentially a complete and utter mystery. We don't even know where 'Sheba' is – although there's a certain amount of evidence to support the suggestion that it may have been the state now known to archaeologists as 'Saba', in the southeastern corner of the Arabian peninsula.

As for the lady herself, apparently, having 'heard of the fame of Solomon concerning the name of the Lord, she came to prove him with hard questions' (10, 1). In search of spiritual guidance, perhaps? In fact, we know much more about the pomp and state in which she arrived ('with a very great train, with camels that bare spices, and very much gold, and precious stones') than we do about her. In the biblical account itself, her glamour and prestige, although taken as read, are only vaguely delineated – she's much more a foil for the grandeur of Solomon's court (10, 6):

And she said to the king, It was a true report that I heard in mine own land of thy acts and of thy wisdom. Howbeit I believed not the words, until I came, and mine eyes had seen it: and, behold, the half was not told me: thy wisdom and prosperity exceedeth the fame which I heard.

Likewise, the lavish presents she and other rulers brought serve as a sort of simile for Solomon's greatness; an assessment of his prestige as measured in material gifts (10, 10):

And she gave the king an hundred and twenty talents of gold, and of spices very great store, and precious stones … And the navy also of Hiram, that brought gold from Ophir, brought in from Ophir great plenty of almug trees, and precious stones.

Most enigmatic of all, given the number, wealth and beauty of Solomon's wives and paramours, is the fact that there's no suggestion of any sexual connection between queen and king in the Bible story. That hasn't stopped the speculation of centuries that Solomon and the Queen of Sheba simply *must* have been royal lovers at the very least.

and beliefs of their own backgrounds. And, indeed, says the Bible (11, 4):

It came to pass, when Solomon was old, that his wives turned away his heart after other gods: and his heart was not perfect with the Lord his God, as was the heart of David his father.

God, in anger, stirred up a series of adversaries against Solomon, so his was to end up an increasingly troubled reign. By the time he died, the unity of Israel had been fatally compromised. His son Rehoboam was able to inherit only the southern realm of Judah. The northern part of the kingdom, as Israel, seceded.

Whips, Scorpions and Elisha

Solomon's relapse into paganism marked a return to the old cycle. Under Rehoboam the decline continued. His reign was inevitably overshadowed by the break-up of his father's kingdom; his policies dominated by the desire to reunite the two realms, if necessary by force. In place of his father's firmness, his subjects found tyranny. 'Whereas my father did lade you with a heavy yoke,' he told them (12, 11), 'I will add to your yoke: my father hath chastised you with whips, but I will chastise you with scorpions.'

Solomon loved were 'strange'. The word, used here, does not of course mean 'odd', 'eccentric' or 'unusual', but foreign – they were literally strangers to Israel and its ways. One, we're told, was the Egyptian Pharaoh's daughter (11, 1); in addition there were 'women of the Moabites, Ammonites, Edomites, Zidonians, and Hittites'.

Such women were a threat in that, however dutiful they were towards their Jewish master, they all brought with them the culture

Rehoboam's son Abijah, and *his* son Asa, were no more successful in restoring David and Solomon's kingdom. Under Jehosophat (Asa's son), Judah tilted once again towards idolatry. A new prophet emerged – Elisha. He called on God to punish his people in their disloyalty and wickedness. God responded by burning up one of the king's captains and his 50 men with a bolt of fire (2 Kings 1, 12). Elisha was by no means done. One day, walking by Bethel, some little children came up and mocked him for his baldness (2, 23):

And he turned back, and looked on them, and cursed them in the name of the Lord. And there came forth two she bears out of the wood, and tare forty and two children of them.

Elisha went on to condemn an insubordinate servant and all his line in perpetuity to leprosy (5, 27) and to get God to smite the entire Syrian people with blindness in punishment for their king's refusal to see the spiritual truth.

An Unlikely Instrument

In the northern kingdom of Israel, the pendulum-swing between pagan deities like Baal and God or Yahweh intensified. Under King Ahab, Baal became the deity of choice. Working

Below: There are times when, to the modern reader, the morality of the Bible seems simply unfathomable. Here forty-two children are torn apart by bears – for mocking Elisha's baldness. God's Prophet was not to be disrespected.

PAINTED LADY

FROM THE DISOBEDIENCE of Eve to the strictures of St Paul, the Bible doesn't stint in its condemnation of the (many, various and major) faults it finds in women. Few of the fair sex, however, have been so savagely vilified over the centuries as Jezebel, the epitome of all that's wrong with women.

Actually reading about her in the Bible, though, is anticlimactic. Not because she's admirable in beliefs and character – far from it. Jezebel, the wife of Ahab, was a tireless advocate for paganism, encouraging her husband to abandon Yahweh for the cult of Baal.

But if this lends a certain credence to Jehu's accusation of 'witchcrafts' against her (9, 22), there's no attempt to suggest that the 'whoredoms' he charges her with are real. Only if we're going to accept that any woman whose attitudes or behaviour we in any way dislike has by virtue of this fact committed 'whoredom'.

Or if we're going to take the view that any sort of personal adornment in a woman is sinful, for it's true that we're told that when she heard Jehu was approaching her palace, Jezebel 'painted her face, and tired her head, and looked out at a window' (9, 30). Jehu, taking possession of the palace, had her thrown from a window: he 'trode her underfoot' before leaving her body where it lay, to be torn apart and eaten by dogs. 'The carcase of Jezebel shall be as dung upon the face of the field', he swore (9, 37), 'so that they shall not say, This is Jezebel.'

A cruel fate, although perhaps no more than she deserved as God's sworn enemy. One thing is certain, though: Jezebel was no 'Jezebel'.

> 'Few of the fair sex have been so savagely vilified over the centuries as Jezebel, the epitome of all that's wrong with women'.

in his mysterious ways, God made Jehosophat's son Jehu his instrument: he ousted King Jehoram, seizing power in a coup. He murdered the king in cold blood, taking his bow and unleashing an arrow that lodged in Jehoram's heart; Jehoram's heir apparent Ahaziah was only wounded but died soon after. In all, Jehu had 70 princes killed (10, 7) to consolidate his power.

As far as we can guess, Jehu's embracing of God's work was opportunistic at best, but there is no doubt that he did much damage to the pagan cause. The House of Ahab, at whose expense he was rising, had invested heavily in the cult of Baal. It made sense for Jehu to attack the temple of the god. 'Go in, and slay them,' he told his troops (10, 25):

'Let none come forth.' And they smote them with the edge of the sword; and the guard and the captains cast them out … And they brought forth the images out of the house of Baal, and burned them. And they brake down the image of Baal, and brake down the house of Baal … Thus Jehu destroyed Baal out of Israel.

Fighting On

The smiting continued more or less unabated. Amaziah, King of Judah, went to war with Edom and slew 10,000 in the 'Valley of Salt'

(14, 7). Meanwhile, Menahem of Israel attacked the rebellious town of Tiphsah (believed to have been somewhere in what is now Syria or southeastern Turkey). Menahem added a new refinement to the traditional repertoire of slaughter (15, 16): 'All the women therein that were with child, he ripped up.' Not to be outdone, the Angel of the Lord himself killed 185,000 Assyrians (19, 35) – although these were, in fairness, invaders threatening Jerusalem.

Right: Jezebel is thrown from her window to be trodden underfoot and devoured by the dogs of the palace, on Jehu's orders. Just punishment (apparently) for forsaking the one true God for the cult of Baal.

Below: The Nuremberg Bible's view of God's vengeance on Assyria (2 Kings 19) naturally gives centre-stage to the Angel of the Lord – but what are we to make of those (Israelite?) sawyers setting to in the background?

EMPIRES OF OPPRESSION

In the ancient Middle East, the Jews we know from scripture had to fight for their freedom from great empires whose stories we're more familiar with from historical and archaeological records.

◆

'The Lord turned not from the fierceness of his great wrath.'
2 KINGS 23, 26.

Merneptah reigned over Egypt from 1213 to 1203 BCE, the fourth Pharaoh of the Nineteenth Dynasty. The pyramids were already ancient by this time. Merneptah's name meant 'Beloved of Ptah' (Ptah was the creator-god), and it was in 1896 that the distinguished Egyptologist Flinders Petrie found a stele – an inscribed

Opposite: Jerusalem, in Ezekiel's vision, had been endowed with all the blessings a city might have had: its buildings were beautiful, its surroundings fertile. Its destruction by the Assyrians (top) was the punishment for its godlessness.

stone monument – to his memory at Thebes. The inscription focuses on Merneptah's defeat of the Libyans. 'A prodigious deed has been done for Egypt,' it concludes. A mighty general, Merneptah:

gave courage to his armies in their hundreds of thousands, restored the breath to those who panted in their fear ... he vanquished the Libyans and sent them packing from Egyptian soil: now the fear of Egypt is deep within their hearts. Their vanguard was routed; their legs would serve them only for flight; their bowmen threw down their weapons in fear; running for their lives, their morale failed them and they discarded their water-skins and kitbags to speed their flight. The Libyan leader, basest of men, ran for his life through the darkness of the night, without his regal headdress – or even the sandals from his feet. Without food or water he fled, fearful of the anger of his own family and of his generals, now turning on one another, their tents reduced to ashes, their supplies seized by our men. No hero's welcome awaited him at home but fear and loathing for a leader marked out as unlucky, damned to defeat by the power of Egypt's Pharaoh…

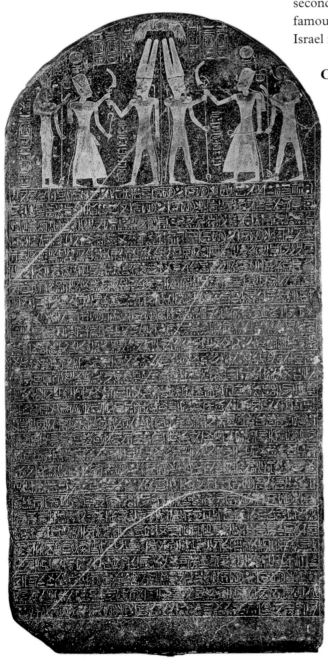

Left: On the so-called 'Israel Stele' (c. 1208 BCE), Israel is actually little more than an afterthought: a peripheral concern for the Pharaoh Merneptah; one of the small-fry nations of the ancient world.

After this signal triumph, the stele sums up other aspects of Merneptah's legacy:

Canaan weeps in her captivity; Ashkelon has been taken and Gezer seized. Yanoam no longer endures; Israel lies devastated, bereft of its seed.

And there we have it – last on a list of the secondary achievements of a now-not-very-famous Pharaoh: the first known mention of Israel in any non-scriptural history.

Chronicled Collisions

Most modern scholars – even believers – would agree that those who think of the Old Testament as literally 'true' are mistaking its original purpose. But so too are those who have it down as a work of fiction – as even the most sceptical researchers would accept. Regardless of religious truth, whether we see the Bible as divine 'revelation' or merely 'myth', there's a historical strand in the scripture that simply cannot be dismissed. In this great drama of the Jews and their destiny, Israel, its tribes, its kings and prophets may have centre-stage, but there are also walk-on parts for some of the most illustrious civilizations of the ancient world. Or march-in parts, perhaps – for these great empires generally arrived as invaders, irrupting their way into Jewish history by force of arms.

Opposite: Prisoners are kept hard at work at a time when Assyria's kings were masters of the ancient world. Enslaved enemies of this kind very likely built the wall in Sennacherib's Palace in Nineveh, on which this relief (c. 700 BCE) appears.

The Assyrians whose forces were laid low by the Angel of Death in 2 Kings 19, 35 were just one example: their King Sennacherib is as well known to ancient historians and archaeologists as he is to biblical scholars. So too, however, were the Hittites, Achaemenid Persia and the Babylonians: all had their different dealings with the Jews, all recorded (from an Israelite perspective) in the Bible.

of separate – and sometimes wildly varying – sources. If these were brought together by ancient scholars, it was for the broader themes and preoccupations they shared – not because they can be seen as constituting the consecutive 'chapters' of a single, straightforward narrative.

A Chaotic Chronology

It's ironic that, just as history makes its first appearance in the Bible narrative, that narrative should go into just about complete chronological meltdown. In the first five books, the so-called 'Pentateuch' (Genesis, Exodus, Leviticus, Numbers and Deuteronomy), the stories may be extravagant and the lifespans (such as Methuselah's 969 years) even more so – but the basic timeline of the action is quite clear.

As the Old Testament goes on, however, we find a clearer sense of narrative unclarity emerging: a realization that we're reading a collection

Right: Though written by Samaritans, this seventeenth-century scroll of the Pentateuch (the Bible's first five books) is believed to represent a link in an unbroken chain of scriptural succession dating all the way back to Old Testament times.

(Just to add to the confusion, the King James Bible differs in its ordering from the traditional Hebrew version – while the Catholic book parts company again.)

Hence, in the King James Bible, we find the Book of Esther – set in the years of Persian power – coming well before the Book of Daniel,

> ## '200,150 people of high and low estate, both men and women were taken captive'.
>
> 2 KINGS 19

which deals with the Babylonian Captivity. An inversion, then, of the historical chronology. The Captivity is a complication in itself, since so many different Prophets wanted to have their say about its significance. The Books of Jeremiah, Hosea, Isaiah and others all address the destruction of Jerusalem and the carrying of Israel into exile, but their placing in the Bible may seem to imply a narrative progression that isn't there. And then there's the Song of Solomon, whose very name suggests a much earlier origin than its final placing in the scriptural sequence seems to imply.

Modern scholars have done their best, but these aren't difficulties that can easily be overcome. This book just tries to find the clearest way it can through a very tangled story.

Incidental Israel

As far as the chronicles of conventional history are concerned, it is Israel that is the occasional interloper, the passing mention – barely registered in other, much grander narratives. In so far as it does occur, the differences of perspective are so striking that we do well to recognize the biblical account at all. Which narration is nearest to the historical truth

is impossible to verify: how are we to judge between Jewish ancestral myth and, say, Assyrian propaganda? Take the invasion of Sennacherib – or, as his own chroniclers called him:

Sennacherib the great, the magnificent world-ruler, King of Assyria and of the four quarters of the world. Wise shepherd to his people; beloved of the gods; protector of right, overseer of justice; friend of the poor; pious in his offices; great hero, strong warrior, foremost among princes. He whose rage destroys the rebellious, whose thunderbolt fells the wicked …

We saw his invasion being summarily dispatched by God's angel in 2 Kings 19. But his own inscriptions recall it rather differently:

Hezekiah of Judah would not bow down to me. Forty-six of his strongholds – all walled cities – as well as innumerable smaller towns in his territory were taken. My men brought up siege-engines, razed them to the ground with battering-rams, attacked and took them by storm, stole in through breaches made in the surrounding walls or undermined their fortifications with mines and tunnels. One way or another, I laid siege to them and took them. 200,150 people of high and low estate, both men and women were taken captive. I carried off as booty countless horses, mules, asses, camels, cattle and sheep. The King himself was holed up in his royal city, caught like a bird in a cage. I built ramps and fortifications to prevent people from leaving the city, imprisoning them in their wretchedness. Having sacked his [other] cities, I cut them off from their hinterlands … The glory of my greatness overwhelmed Hezekiah in his terror: the Arabs and other mercenaries who had come to serve him deserted him. In the end he had to submit to my yoke and to pay me tribute: 30 talents of gold; 800 talents of silver; gems; antimony; jewels; carnelian; couches and chairs inlaid with ivory; elephant hides and tusks; ebony, boxwood and other rich treasures, along with his daughters, his wives, his musicians – men and women … All these things I had brought to me in Nineveh.

A close reading confirms that, despite these triumphs, Hezekiah's capital wasn't taken (although other sources suggest that this was because he had to return to Assyria to deal with an attempted coup). There's no mention of an Israelite victory, though – nor of any angelic intervention. Otherwise, much of Sennacherib's account rings true.

Assyria seems for the most part to have been content to take the tribute of its subject states. Sennacherib would have seen no need to plant his banner on the battlements of Jerusalem, or to stay in occupation of the conquered country as long as its Jewish rulers paid their tax.

The Assyrian Empire

The city-state of Assur stood on the western side of the River Tigris in the northern part of what is now Iraq. The rich and fertile floodplains of the Tigris and Euphrates formed the area we now know as Mesopotamia – the name coming from a Greek phrase meaning 'between the rivers'. Mesopotamia had long since been a crucial 'cradle of civilization': great states like those of Sumer and Babylon had sprung up in the Delta region to the south. (Abraham, the Jewish patriarch, hailed from Ur, a Sumerian city.)

By about 1350 BCE, however, the northern part of Mesopotamia was under the control of Assur – the Assyrian Empire had emerged, built by ferocious warrior-kings like Shalmaneser I. Expanding out of the river valleys into the hill-country of Anatolia, he had broken the power of the Hittites there. That first Assyrian Empire had faltered, in the final decades of the first millennium – a 'Dark Age' of chaos and imperial collapse and chaos across the Middle East and

Seated in splendour, as befits a conqueror, Sennacherib receives the reports of his generals after his successful siege of Lachish, in Judah, 701 BCE. He hadn't taken Jerusalem, but hadn't needed to: the whole kingdom was effectively under his control.

Mediterranean – but its fortunes were restored by the conquering kings of the tenth century BCE. Ashurnasirpal II (883–59 BCE) built a splendid new imperial capital at Nineveh, while his son and successor Shalmaneser III (859–24 BCE) invaded Israel, exacting tribute from King Jehu. By the time Sennacherib was on the throne (he reigned from 705 to 681 BCE), Assyria was the dominant power in the Middle East.

Above: A moment's cordiality in what was ultimately to be a stormy history: King Shalmaneser III (right) greets a Babylonian ruler. In the ninth century BCE, the balance of power lay firmly with the Assyrians; soon, however, their positions were to be reversed.

Assyrian Fall, Babylonian Rise

By the end of the seventh century BCE, however, Assyrian power was waning. Babylon was in the ascendant now. Established almost a millennium before in 1894 BCE, it had been one of a number of southern city-states jostling for prominence in Mesopotamia. It had even briefly had an empire under King Hammurabi in the eighteenth century BCE. It had quickly been eclipsed under his successors, though, and in thrall to Assyrian power for centuries thereafter. But at the end of the seventh century BCE it was resurgent. Ashurbanipal of Assyria had died some time around 627 BCE, and none of his successors seemed quite equal to the task of leading.

> 'Assisted by bloody succession wars within the Assyrian elite, Nabopolassar expanded his territories northward'.

King Nabopolassar, who had come to the throne of Babylon soon after Ashurbanipal's death in 625 BCE, didn't just throw off the yoke but he smashed Assyrian power altogether. Assisted by bloody succession wars within the Assyrian elite, Nabopolassar expanded his territories northward. Around 612 BCE, he laid siege to Nineveh with an enormous army. After three months the city fell – and with it Assyrian power.

The Glory of Babylon

Nebuchadnezzar's capital was already legendary in its magnificence, with its gigantic ziggurats (Mesopotamian terraced pyramids) and its majestic walls. Imposing as these fortifications were, they were dwarfed by the splendour of the Ishtar gate, named in honour of the ancient Semitic goddess of love, war, fertility and sex, its blue-tiled turrets adorned with lions, bulls and dragons. Further sculptures lined the processional way that ran beneath.

'The thickness of the wall is thirty-two feet', wrote the Greek traveller Strabo (albeit some

Below: A conflagration – and lamentations: the face of the ancient world was seemingly changed when (around 612 BCE) Nineveh fell to Nabopolassar's Babylonian siege; in reality, though, Assyrian power had been waning for some time.

centuries later): two four-horse chariots could pass each other on the walkway along its top.

Dedicated to the fertility god, Marduk, the Etemenanki Ziggurat is believed to have stood

over 90m (295ft) tall in the city's heyday. It rose up in seven tiers, with a little temple at the top.

Here too could apparently be found the 'Hanging Gardens of Babylon' – although what this wonder actually comprised is a matter of speculation. What they were perhaps hardly matters: suffice it to say that Nebuchadnezzar's Babylon was by general acknowledgement the most spectacular city the world had ever seen.

Below: The world had never seen the like of Babylon – its power, its wealth and the glory that it blazoned forth with incredible constructions like its 'Hanging Gardens', its ziggurats, its temples and its Ishtar Gate (below).

Josiah's Gamble

All around the region, watching rulers saw an opportunity to step into the power vacuum that Assyria's collapse appeared to have opened up. Judah had been growing in strength and confidence since the accession of King Josiah in 641 BCE: his fanatical drive to re-establish Yahweh's cult had brought his whole kingdom together in an energizing cause. But he overreached himself when, in the wake of Assyria's fall, he sought to re-create Solomon's United Kingdom of Judah and Israel.

In 605 BCE, knowing that Necho II was marching his army eastward to offer his Assyrian ally assistance against the Babylonians, Josiah

Above: King Josiah overreached himself in his plans to reunite the Jewish kingdoms – and his bid to outfox the Pharaoh Necho II. His death at Megiddo (605 BCE) put an end to his manoeuvrings – and put little Judah firmly in its place.

resolved to prevent them from getting through. His idea was that he would intercept the Egyptians as they crossed a narrow pass outside the city of Megiddo, southeast of Haifa: in those rugged uplands, the Jews should have the advantage of surprise.

In the event, Josiah's plan worked to the extent that he was able to get his army into position, but the advancing Egyptians simply swept his forces aside. If the biblical account

THE JUSTICE OF JUDITH

ANGRY AT ISRAEL'S rebellious spirit, King Nebuchadnezzar called his general Holofernes to him: he ordered him to take a vast army and subjugate the country once and for all. So Holofernes set out and, marching upon the kingdom, quickly started making inroads on its territory: Israel's military force was reeling, its menfolk truly cowed.

But a beautiful young widow named Judith was not quite so easily intimidated. She felt frustrated at her people's passivity – and their lack of faith in God. Deciding to take action, she set forth with her waiting-woman and sought out the enemy camp. She wanted, she told the guards at the gate, to see their General Holofernes. She could give him tips on how to take her country, without further losses on his side. Hearing her words – and, more to the point, seeing her surpassing beauty – they took her to see Holofernes in his tent. Delighted to have such an appealing guest, he dined with her, drank and flirted; she flattered his attentions and encouraged his expectations.

As the night grew late, his attendants left discreetly so as not to breach their master's privacy. Lulled to sleepiness, Holofernes nodded, at which point Judith grabbed his sword: seizing his head by the hair, she swung hard and severed his neck completely. With her waiting-woman's help, she stuffed Holofernes' head in a bag and they both fled.

They took their trophy to the Israelite camp to show it to the soldiers, so they could see that their enemy might be vanquished – and by the wiles of woman.

One of the more peculiar not-quite-biblical texts that proliferated in Old Testament times, the Book of Judith stands out for the unsettling power of its story. Excluded from the King James and other Protestant Bibles (although it's always made it into Catholic versions), it is believed to have been written relatively late, long after the events it purports to describe.

Although the invading king is referred to as Nebuchadnezzar, he is also described as an Assyrian ruler. Holofernes' army, indeed, sets out from Nineveh. In the end, most scholars have concluded that Nebuchadnezzar is more a generic oppressor of Jewish custom and culture. And his general Holofernes is, all agree, a most unfortunate man.

Mankind – or manhood – is arguably the 'real' victim in one of those ancient texts that seems positively to cry out for modern Freudian interpretation. Judith in her deadly eroticism sums up all that is most alluring – and most dangerous – in womankind. In that strange symbolic logic by which decapitation seems no more than a metaphor for the (somehow scarier) menace of castration, the story's climactic moment is not Holofernes' beheading but something 'worse'.

(2 Chronicles 35, 23) is to be believed, Josiah was killed by an archer.

As for the power vacuum, that never really came about. Granted, marching on to Mesopotamia the Pharaoh was defeated by

Nabopolassar's Babylonians at Carchemish. But Josiah was no longer there to take advantage. Nor was his son and successor, Jehoahaz, able to follow through, since he was deposed by Necho on his homeward journey.

He was replaced by his younger and more tractable brother, Jehoiakim. Egypt was now the real power in Palestine.

A Reckless Throw

If he had an overlord in the Pharaoh, Jehoiakim reasoned, he surely had a powerful ally as well. When Nabopolassar's son Nebuchadnezzar, having vanquished Assyria, demanded the tribute Judah had hitherto paid to Nineveh, Jehoiakim was emboldened to refuse.

In 597 BCE, Babylonian forces took Jerusalem after a three-month siege. Leading members of Judah's elite were taken off to the conquerors' capital to live in exile (2 Kings 24, 14):

And he carried away all Jerusalem, and all the princes, and all the mighty men of valour, even ten thousand captives, and all the craftsmen and smiths.

What amounted to large-scale hostage-taking seems to have been fairly common practice at the time: groups of important administrators had been taken back to Nineveh by the Assyrians. These earlier experiences, however, don't seem to have seared themselves on to the Jewish consciousness in quite the same way as this 'Babylonian Captivity'.

Nebuchadnezzar left a client prince, Zedekiah, in charge of Judah. But the spirit of rebellion was to prove infectious. In 588 BCE, it was Zedekiah's turn to rise up in revolt. This time Nebuchadnezzar showed no mercy.

Below: Judith draws a cloth cover over the decapitated corpse of Holofernes. The fascination of her story lies in its juxtaposition of 'ladylike' comportment and 'feminine' charm and more rough-and-ready fears – of castration and of death.

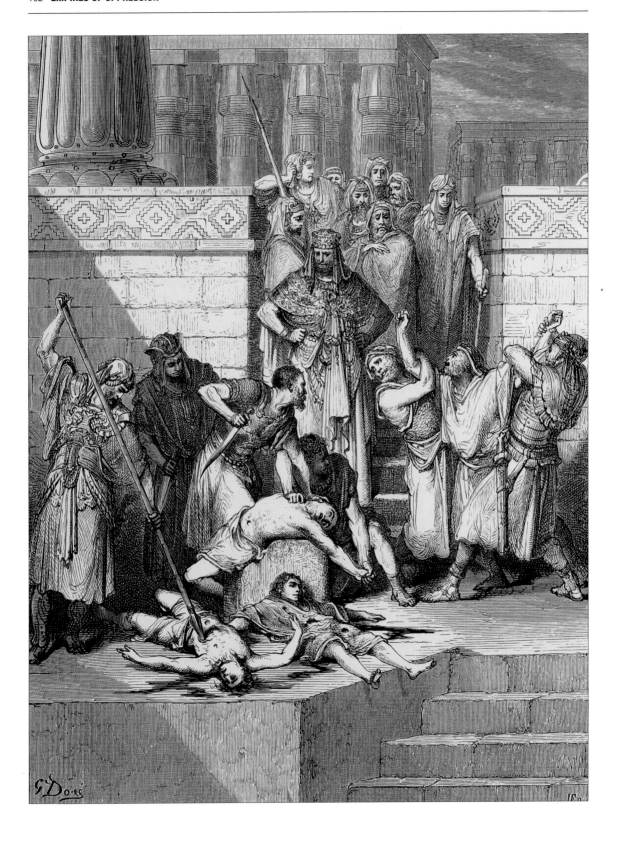

Opposite: Zedekiah's sons are slaughtered by the troops of Nebuchadnezzar II. A client king who rebelled against his overlord, Zedekiah could expect no clemency from the Babylonians, who blinded him and bore him off in chains.

The following year his armies attacked in overwhelming force: they ravaged Judah and razed Jerusalem – and its temple – to the ground. 'The city was broken up,' reports the Second Book of Kings (25, 4), 'And they slew the sons of Zedekiah before his eyes.' And that grisly sight was to be the last the king beheld. For the Babylonians promptly 'put out the eyes of Zedekiah, and bound him with fetters of brass, and carried him to Babylon' (25, 7).

Another wave of deportations tore the heart out of the kingdom: only the poorest and least powerful remained.

Beautiful Harlots

'How doth the city sit solitary, that was full of people,' opens the biblical book of The Lamentations of Jeremiah (Lamentations 1, 1). Like a widow, 'she weepeth sore in the night, and her tears are on her cheeks.' But it isn't long before the emphasis is shifting; the unfortunate widow being blamed for misfortunes that it now seems she's brought upon herself because, apparently, 'Jerusalem hath grievously sinned'. She has cheapened herself, says the prophet, by her sluttishness (1, 8):

All that honoured her despise her, because they have seen her nakedness … Her filthiness is in her skirts.

So beloved was Jerusalem to the Old Testament prophets, it appears, that its attractions could only adequately be evoked in the imagery of feminine beauty. Unfortunately, its fall was seen in feminine terms as well. While it's obviously assumed that God's is an equal-opportunities anger, moved as much by the wrongdoing of Jewish men, it was the idea of the fallen woman that gripped the imagination.

Above: Ezekiel described his beloved city as a beautiful but unworthy woman. The 'Babylonian Captivity' gave the Jews everything from a newly-distinct identity to a rich literature of exile and of longing.

Ezekiel, one of the exiles, was poetic in his denunciations of his people. The city of Jerusalem, in his vision, had been beloved of God as a beautiful woman might be of a man. He had showered her with gifts, he said (Ezekiel 16, 10):

I clothed thee also with broidered work, and shod thee with badgers' skin, and I girded thee about with fine linen, and I covered thee with silk. I decked thee also with ornaments, and I put bracelets upon thy hands, and a chain on thy neck. And I put a jewel on thy forehead, and earrings in thine ears, and a beautiful crown upon thine head.

But she had proven unworthy, unfaithful in her 'abominations' and her 'whoredoms'

JUDAISM: MADE IN MESOPOTAMIA

THE EXPERIENCE OF exile in Babylon was at once a culture shock and a source of sadness, but it was in many ways to be the making of the Jews. Here, transported to a foreign land, they had no alternative but to reinterpret their religion as a creed, a set of traditions and beliefs, rather than a local – and highly place-specific – cult. Instead of Solomon's Temple, they had now to make do with a generic place-of-worship, a synagogue. Paradoxically, though, this solemnified the act of prayer. The synagogue might never be able to match the sanctity of the Temple in Jerusalem – but this just made the community of worshippers more crucial.

Laws on food and hygiene, once perhaps little more than a code of guidance for the super-scrupulous, became a daily reminder of a Jew's identity. That identity was being internalized, installed in the psychology of the individual Jew and in his or her community feeling: the Prophet Ezekiel began to talk of a Jerusalem that was more an image, an emblem than an actual home. (To this day, accordingly, Jews offer the wistful prayer 'Next year in Jerusalem' – although of course they can be there the next day by simply getting on a plane.)

As enduring as its legacy has been, the Babylonian Captivity was quite short. In 539 BCE, Babylon was conquered by the Persians, whose emperor Cyrus II ('the Great') authorized the Jews to return to their homes. Not only that, but he offered his help in the reconstruction of the Temple. Even so, the decades of exile had altered the Jews, and their religion, irrevocably: had they not been compelled to spend this time in exile, much of what we understand as Judaism would never have evolved; the Jews might have been a nation just like any other.

Left: Another bloody battle: for the Jews, though, the Fall of Babylon brought redemption. Cyrus the Great of Persia didn't simply free them from their old oppressors, he rebuilt the Temple of Jerusalem on their behalf.

(16, 22). A 'harlot' (16, 35), she had betrayed her husband, giving her gifts to all who asked. 'Thus saith the Lord God' (said Ezekiel):

Because thy filthiness was poured out, and thy nakedness discovered through thy whoredoms with thy lovers, and with all the idols of thy abominations, and by the blood of thy children, which thou didst give unto them (16, 36).

This same story was to be acted out almost exactly in the Book of Hosea, in which the prophet married Gomer, 'a wife of whoredoms' (Hosea 1, 2). He did so on the Lord's instructions – seemingly so that the resulting story of disappointment, pain and anger could serve as a metaphor for God's disillusion

Below: History gives us no reason to think that Nebuchadnezzar II died any way other than peacefully and in his Babylonian bed. As far as the Bible is concerned, however, he ended his days in the wilderness in insane animal-hood.

with Israel in a time when they were once more unfaithfully flirting with the beliefs and practices of pagan worship (4, 12):

The spirit of whoredoms hath caused them to err, and they have gone a whoring from under their God. They sacrifice upon the tops of the mountains, and burn incense upon the hills, under oaks and poplars and elms ...

Pride and Punishment

Babylon's prosperity was too exorbitant, its pride too overreaching, not to be brought low. The arrogance of Nebuchadnezzar outran his many great achievements. One day, as he was walking through his palace, exulting at the great wealth and splendour that he saw around him, he asked aloud 'Is not this great Babylon, that I have built for the house of the kingdom by the might of my power, and for the honour of my majesty?' (Daniel 4, 30). Even as the

word was in his mouth, a voice from heaven challenged him:

O king Nebuchadnezzar, to thee it is spoken; The kingdom is departed from thee. And they shall drive thee from men, and thy dwelling shall be with the beasts of the field; they shall make thee to eat grass as oxen ...

Within an hour, he was out in the wilderness, eating grass, his body 'wet with the dew of heaven, till his hairs were grown like eagles'

> 'Belshazzar made a great feast to a thousand of his lords, and drank wine before the thousand'.
>
> DANIEL 5, 1

feathers, and his nails like birds' claws' (4, 33).

A grotesque end to Nebuchadnezzar's ambition, then, but Babylonian power was not yet finished. History has Babylon being gradually overshadowed by the power of Persia rising to the east. But the Bible, typically, offers us a tale of overweening pride and catastrophic fall in the (perhaps not wholly mythical) figure of King Belshazzar.

A Feast and a Fright

Belshazzar, we're told (5, 1):

made a great feast to a thousand of his lords, and drank wine before the thousand. Belshazzar, whiles he tasted the wine, commanded to bring the golden and silver vessels which his father Nebuchadnezzar had taken out of the temple which was in Jerusalem; that the king, and his princes, his wives, and his concubines, might drink therein.

Right: The writing is – terrifyingly – on the wall for King Belshazzar and for Babylon. The use of the sacred utensils of the Jews for feasting has sealed his empire's fate after a reign of overweening arrogance and oppression.

The sacrilege was compounded by the company's using these vessels for the toasting of their pagan gods – their figures 'of gold, and of silver, of brass, of iron, of wood, and of stone' (5, 4).

'In the same hour', the story famously continues:

came forth fingers of a man's hand, and wrote over against the candlestick upon the plaister of the wall of the king's palace: and the king saw the part of the hand that wrote. Then the king's countenance was changed, and his thoughts troubled him, so that the joints of his loins were loosed, and his knees smote one against another.

The message was written in mysterious characters: unable to read it, the king cried out for his astrologers and soothsayers, but they were no more able to decipher it than he had been. Then his queen recalled the presence in his kingdom of a man named Daniel, one of the Jewish exiles in Babylon.

Belshazzar had Daniel summoned, offering him sumptuous rewards if he could read the message, but the prophet told him to keep them: he would interpret free of charge. The message was quite clear, he said: Belshazzar had known of Nebuchadnezzar's fate – driven from the sons of men to live in beasthood. Far from heeding its warning, however, he had only outdone his predecessor's pride. In this latest blasphemy, in drinking from God's holy vessels to do honour to his idols, he had lifted himself up against the Lord of Heaven (5, 23).

'This', said Daniel, 'is the writing that was written, MENE, MENE, TEKEL, UPHARSIN' (5, 25). And this was 'the interpretation of the thing': God, he said, had set a limit on his kingship, 'and finished it'. 'Thou art weighed in the balances, and art found wanting,' he went on. Belshazzar's realm was now divided, and was 'given to the Medes and Persians'. That night, indeed, Belshazzar was killed, and 'Darius the Median' took his kingdom. The glories of Babylon had come to a bitter end.

A Persian Protector

The biblical account sits a little uneasily with that of secular history here. The Persians (a people whose rulers had early on formed familial alliances with their former overlords, the Medes) did indeed overwhelm Babylonia at about this time. And there was to be an Emperor Darius – although not until some time later. Darius the Mede has his only

Left: Daniel deciphers the words which were written by the moving hand at Belshazzar's Feast: the King, cast down, can only mourn his impending doom; the fact that he has been 'weighed in the balances, and ... found wanting'.

Right: Cyrus the Great, enthroned in Babylon, gives the order for the Jews to be set free and returned to their home where, with his help, they will be able to rebuild their ruined Temple.

IN THE LIONS' DEN

DARIUS, THE BIBLE tells us, had come to love his leading official, Daniel, but became enraged when – after he had issued an imperial prohibition – Daniel insisted on continuing to say his Hebrew prayers. So furious was Darius that he allowed his advisers to persuade him to cast Daniel into a pit or dungeon in his palace that he kept furnished with a pride of lions.

That night the Emperor could not speak for his guilt at how he had treated an official he loved as a friend; first thing in the morning, then, he hastened to the lions' den. There, crying out to Daniel 'with a lamentable voice' (Daniel 6, 20), he 'spake and said to Daniel':

O Daniel, servant of the living God, is thy God, whom thou servest continually, able to deliver thee from the lions? Then said Daniel unto the king, O king, live for ever. My God hath sent his angel, and hath shut the lions' mouths, that they have not hurt me: forasmuch as before him innocency was found in me; and also before thee, O king, have I done no hurt.

Now it was the turn of those who had denounced Daniel to be thrown into the lions' den on Darius' orders – not just his advisers but 'their children, and their wives' (6, 24). They did not enjoy the Lord's protection:

and the lions had the mastery of them and brake all their bones in pieces or ever they came at the bottom of the den.

mention in the Book of Daniel: it was he who, famously, falling out with Daniel, whom he had made his official, had him thrown into the lion's den.

As far as history is concerned, the conqueror of Babylon (in 539 BCE) was Cyrus II – Cyrus

---

> 'My God hath sent his angel, and hath shut the lions' mouths, that they have not hurt me'.
>
> DANIEL 6, 22

---

the Great. His Achaemenid dynasty, named after a semi-mythical seventh-century BCE ancestor, King Achaemenes, was to dominate the Middle East for a couple of centuries. (It was also, of course, to make its mark on the history of classical Greece.)

Cyrus, although a conqueror, was hardly an oppressor. Like other imperialists of his time, he was happy enough to administer his realms at arm's length through a system of satraps, or client kings. As for his treatment of the Jews, whether out of altruism or political calculation he acted well enough to be afterwards acclaimed as a 'Messiah'.

His Jewish subjects had no doubt at all that 'the Lord stirred up the spirit of Cyrus' (2 Chronicles 36, 22). 'He made a proclamation throughout all his kingdom, and put it also in writing, saying' (36, 23):

Thus saith Cyrus king of Persia, All the kingdoms of the earth hath the Lord God of heaven given me; and he hath charged me to build him an house in Jerusalem, which is in Judah.

Cyrus didn't just bring an end to the Babylonian Captivity, in other words, allowing the exiles to return to their homeland: he rebuilt the Temple that Nebuchadnezzar had destroyed.

Esther, Queen of Persia

Ahasuerus, better known in western history by the name the Greeks gave him, Xerxes, ruled over a vast proportion of the ancient world. He also, in his wife Vashti, had possession of one of its most exquisite prizes. Her breathtaking beauty added lustre to his reign. And so he liked to show her off: one day, says the Book of Esther (1, 11), he summoned her from a banquet she was giving for women visitors to the kingdom, so that his guests could see her beauty and envy him. Whether through vanity and disobedience or (as modern feminists have suggested) a feisty independence of spirit, Vashti 'refused to come at the king's commandment' and the king was 'wroth', or angry. So much so that he put aside his wife and sent out his messengers across his

Below: Thrown into the lions' den by the angry Darius, the Prophet Daniel is left unscathed. The Angel of the Lord shuts the lions' mouths. His 'innocency', the fact that he has 'done no hurt', is his protection.

A SONG OF SEX

SUPPOSEDLY THE WORK of Solomon, the Song of Songs is a loosely constructed dialogue between two lovers. A work of transporting passion and poetic beauty, there's nothing 'dark' about it, but to more puritanical readers it's often seemed oddly un-scriptural in its celebration of sexual love and longing.

'A bundle of myrrh is my wellbeloved unto me,' says the woman (Song of Songs 1, 13): 'He shall lie all night betwixt my breasts.' 'By night on my bed I sought him whom my soul loveth: I sought him, but I found him not' (3, 1). 'O daughters of Jerusalem, if ye find my beloved, that ye tell him, that I am sick of love' (5, 8).

Her man is every bit as lovestruck (4, 11):

Thy lips, O my spouse, drop as the honeycomb; honey and milk are under thy tongue; and the smell of thy garments is like the smell of Lebanon. A garden inclosed is my sister, my spouse; a spring shut up, a fountain sealed.

He comes to see her at her home and a veritable flurry of innuendo ensues (5, 4):

My beloved put in his hand by the hole of the door, and my bowels were moved for him. I rose up to open to my beloved; and by hands dropped with myrrh, and my fingers with sweet smelling myrrh … I opened to my beloved.

Ultimately, the darkest thing about the Song of Songs is its appreciation of the sheer (and potentially destructive) power of desire – a power that is not readily to be held in check (8, 6):

Love is as strong as death; jealousy is as cruel as the grave: the coals thereof are coals of fire … Many waters cannot quench love, neither can the floods drown it.

empire to bring him 'fair young virgins' from whom he might choose a replacement.

The decision fell on Esther, an orphaned Jewish girl being brought up by her cousin Mordecai, in Susa, Persia's capital. Ahasuerus, unaware that Esther was Jewish, loved her 'above all the women, and she obtained grace and favour in his sight more than all the virgins; so that he set the royal crown upon her head, and made her queen instead of Vashti' (2, 17).

While rivalling her in looks, Esther could hardly have been more different from her predecessor: she was meek and compliant,

utterly self-effacing. When news reached her of a plot to massacre the empire's Jews so that their property could be taken, her cousin called upon her to help, but she was afraid even to approach her husband without his prior summons – an offence in principle punishable by death. In the end, though, she summoned up the courage: going to Ahasuerus she revealed what was afoot – and also her personal stake in what was happening. 'If I have found favour in thy sight,' she said (7, 3):

let my life be given me at my petition, and my people at my request. For we are sold, I and my people, to be destroyed, to be slain, and to perish.

Her husband had the ringleader of the pogrom plot hanged immediately.

A little surprisingly, perhaps, it seems to have been with Ahasuerus' blessing that Esther's

people now carried out their own attacks on their Persian persecutors: they 'slew of their foes seventy and five thousand' across the empire (9, 16). He also authorized Esther's decree, as Queen of Persia, that the Jews from that time forth should celebrate their escape from slaughter with annual 'days of feasting and joy, and of sending portions one to another, and gifts to the poor' (9, 22). The festival of Purim has been honoured ever since.

Nineveh on Notice

As we've seen, the biblical narrative overlapped intriguingly with that of ancient history, but spiritual truth trumped chronological exactitude every time. So it is that we find, in the final books of the Old Testament, accounts of the fall of Nineveh, when the Assyrian collapse had long been – in historical terms – old news.

So it is that the Book of Jonah begins with the prophet receiving his summons from the Lord (1, 2):

Arise, go to Nineveh, that great city, and cry against it; for their wickedness is come up before me.

Jonah, the story goes, attempted to flee his responsibilities and took a sea passage to Tarshish (possibly Sardinia), only to be thwarted by a tempest sent by God. Thrown overboard by his ship's terrified crew, he was famously swallowed by a whale and finally disgorged on dry land, where God gave him a second chance to do his duty.

This time he 'went unto Nineveh, according to the word of the Lord' (3, 3), 'and he cried, and said, Yet forty days, and Nineveh shall be overthrown.' The people heard him, repented their sins, 'proclaimed a fast, and put on

Left: Jonah makes an unconventional landing, coughed up by the whale on the coast of the Aegean to complete his prophetic mission to the people of Nineveh. This scene comes from a fresco at the Greek Orthodox Monastery of Saint Nicholas Anapausas, Meteora, Thessaly.

sackcloth' (3, 5). God had mercy on the city – this time at least.

The Book of Nahum, however, finds God once more 'furious' (1, 1), despite being 'slow to anger' (1, 3). The people of Nineveh had not done their duty to their Lord. A punisher had come who would dash the people to pieces (2,

'The chariots shall rage in the streets, they shall justle one another in the broad ways'.

NAHUM 2, 4

Below: Unfazed by the monuments to Assyrian might all about him in Nineveh, Jonah attacks the faithlessness and immorality he sees about him in the city. Surprisingly, perhaps, he seems to have been given a sympathetic hearing.

1) and an avenging army would descend on the city. The shield of his mighty men is made red, wrote the prophet (2, 3):

the valiant men are in scarlet: the chariots shall be with flaming torches in the day of his preparation, and the fir trees shall be terribly shaken. The chariots shall rage in the streets, they shall justle one against another in the broad ways: they shall seem like torches, they shall run like the lightnings.

'Woe the bloody city!' exclaimed Nahum (3, 1): 'It is all full of lies and robbery.' Accordingly, it could not be allowed to continue in existence. 'O king of Assyria,' he concluded (3, 18):

Thy nobles shall dwell in the dust: thy people is scattered upon the mountains, and no man gathereth them. There is no healing of thy bruise; thy wound is grievous.

Nor could the Assyrians expect sympathy from others:

All that hear the bruit of thee shall clap the hands over thee: for upon whom hath not thy wickedness passed continually?

The Book of Zephaniah agreed (2, 13):

And he will stretch out his hand against the north,

ISRAEL AFFLICTED

ALL THE PROPHETS might in their different ways be said to articulate the tribulations of an Israel feeling abandoned and empty in its alienation from its God, yet oppressed by a succession of much stronger earthly enemies. The Book of Joel is particularly powerful in the mood of devastation it evokes:

That which the palmerworm hath left hath the locust eaten; and that which the locust hath left hath the cankerworm eaten; and that which the cankerworm hath left hath the caterpiller eaten (1, 4).

Is it animal pests or human attackers who have laid this country to waste (1, 6)?

For a nation is come up upon my land, strong, and without number, whose teeth are the teeth of a lion … He hath laid my vine waste, and barked my fig tree; he hath made it clean bare, and cast it away; the branches thereof are made white.

Either way, the land is devastated. In Chapter 2, a locust swarm descends, darkening the sky and galloping across the plains:

A fire devoureth before them; and behind them a flame burneth: the land is as the garden of Eden before them, and behind them a desolate wilderness; yea, and nothing shall escape them. The appearance of them is as the appearance of horses; and as horsemen, so shall they run. Like the noise of chariots on the tops of mountains shall they leap, like the noise of a flame of fire that devoureth the stubble, as a strong people set in battle array … They shall run like mighty men; they shall climb the wall like men of war; and they shall march every one on his ways, and they shall not break their ranks.

and destroy Assyria; and will make Nineveh a desolation, and dry like a wilderness. And flocks shall lie down in the midst of her, all the beasts of the nations.

The great metropolis would become an unpopulated swamp (2, 14):

both the cormorant and the bittern shall lodge in the upper lintels of it; their voice shall sing in the windows; desolation shall be in the thresholds.

'This', said Zephaniah (2, 15), 'is the rejoicing city that dwelt carelessly, that said in her heart, I am, and there is none beside me'. Assyria's capital had become an emblem of human heedlessness and self-involvement.

Right: 'A Prophet is not without honour, save in his own country,' Christ was to say (Mark 6, 4). Jonah found a ready ear in Nineveh. The people there repented of their misdeeds, and God spared their city – for the time being.

'NOT PEACE, BUT A SWORD'

'Love thy neighbour…', 'Turn the other cheek …', 'Blessed are the peacemakers…' Even in Christ's own Gospels, these values sometimes struggle to prevail.

◆

'What manner of child shall this be.' LUKE 1, 66.

The Prophet Jeremiah had given notice that the relationship between the Lord and his Chosen People was eventually destined to change (Jeremiah 31, 31):

Behold, the days come, saith the Lord, that I will make a new covenant with the house of Israel, and with the house of Judah.

The first covenant had been established during the Exodus of Egypt, when God had given Moses his laws – and his promise to support the Jews. Christians hold that a 'New

Covenant' was inaugurated with Christ's offering of the Eucharist at the Last Supper, but by that time his coming had already transformed the relationship between God and man – and, more specifically, the Jews – in the scriptures. The New Testament differs radically from the Old Testament in tone. The word Gospel means 'good news', as the Christians keep reminding us, and there's no disputing the new and unfamiliar emphasis we find in their pages on kindness, tolerance, forgiveness, informality and joy.

For a seriously 'dark history', then, we have to turn to the hypocrisies of Christ's supposed followers in the later Church. But the New Testament does have its darker moments too.

The Holy Innocents

Although, as the province of Judaea, the land of the Jews was in New Testament times a territory

Opposite: Born of the Virgin Mary (above) Christ was to redeem the sins of humankind – but only through his crucifixion and death. Giotto's fresco (opposite) shows him being betrayed, by the kiss of his supposed supporter Judas.

Above: The Three Wise Men appear before King Herod, whose show of enthusiasm at the birth of a new 'King of the Jews' is promptly belied by the Massacre of the Innocents – the slaughter of all male babies – he orders.

of the Roman Empire, it enjoyed a degree of limited autonomy – and its own Jewish ruler, a client-king named Herod.

In Jewish history Herod may have won the honorific 'the Great', for his rebuilding of the Temple, but he's always been the king whom Christians loved to hate. Not surprisingly, perhaps, given his scriptural role: hearing from the three 'wise men from the east' (Matthew 2, 1) that a new 'King of the Jews' had been born, he had begged them to let him know if they should find him (2, 8). When, warned by an

angel, they didn't come back after finding the infant Jesus and went home by a different route, Herod (2, 16):

was exceeding wroth, and sent forth, and slew all the children that were in Bethlehem, and in all the coasts thereof, from two years old and under.

The infant Jesus was not among them, Joseph having been urged by another angel in a dream to take his wife and child away to Egypt for their safety.

Simeon's Sword

'Think not that I am come to send peace on earth,' Christ was to tell his disciples many years later (Matthew 10, 34). 'I came not to send peace, but a sword.' This threat may have been figurative, symbolic, but the all too real threat of violence was to dog his steps his whole life, from the Massacre of the Innocents to his own Passion and Crucifixion.

Meanwhile, safely back in his home country, Jesus was taken to the Temple in Jerusalem by his parents. There he was hailed by a 'just and devout' man (Luke 2, 24), with the Holy Ghost upon him. Simeon had been waiting all his life for the coming of the Messiah, God's 'salvation' (2, 30): 'A light to lighten the Gentiles, and the glory of thy people Israel.' Good news – but

Below: 'It is written, My house shall be called the house of prayer; but ye have made it a den of thieves' (Matthew 21, 13) Christ drives the moneychangers and the traders from the Temple, as imagined by El Greco (c. 1600).

there was a warning too for the boy's mother, Mary: 'Yea, a sword shall pierce through thy own soul also' (2, 35).

For the moment, though, all was well and the boy grew up in apparent peace until the moment came for him to embark on his ministry. Jesus was indeed 'the light of the world' (John 8, 12). The darkness in this part of his story is not easy to find, although we do at least see a flash of temper in Christ's reaction to the commercialization of Jewish worship (Matthew 21, 12):

And Jesus went into the temple of God, and cast out all them that sold and bought in the temple, and overthrew the tables of the moneychangers, and the seats of them that sold doves, And said unto them,

It is written, My house shall be called the house of prayer; but ye have made it a den of thieves.

Joy Shall be in Heaven

Other than this, the story of Christ's ministry is a more or less uninterrupted stream of light. It's not that Jesus doesn't encounter wrongdoers – there's Zacchaeus the tax collector (Luke 9), for instance; the Woman Caught in Adultery (John 8, 3); the repentant woman who knelt weeping and washed Christ's feet with tears (Luke 7, 36). This woman has traditionally been taken to be the Mary Magdalene we meet at Luke 8, 2, although the Gospel doesn't actually state that this is so.

In every case, however, the sinner's appearance only gives Christ the opportunity to show his forgiveness. 'I say unto you,' he tells those who have been listening to his parable of the Good Shepherd, who would not rest until he found the sheep that had strayed (Luke 15, 7):

that likewise joy shall be in heaven over one sinner that repenteth, more than over ninety and nine just persons, which need no repentance.

Thirty Pieces of Silver

Darkness doesn't really enter the Gospel narrative until we read of Christ's betrayal by one of his friends and apostles, Judas Iscariot.

Right: A dutiful daughter, if nothing else, Salome is rewarded for her dancing display by the reward her mother has asked for. The head of John the Baptist is lowered into a pewter plate, in Andrea Solari's painting of 1510.

DANCE OF DEATH

JESUS' OLDER COUSIN John the Baptist had a special status as the man who prepared the way for Christ's coming (Luke 1, 78), and signalled the start of his ministry by baptizing him in the River Jordan (hence his title). That he too fell foul of King Herod had nothing to do with his relationship to the Redeemer – nor, really, anything directly to do with Herod himself. Rather, an outspoken moralist, he had upset the queen, Herodias, with his condemnation of her marriage to the king. (She had previously been married to King Herod's brother Philip.)

Herodias had wanted John the Baptist killed, but her husband had refused, fearing John as 'a just man and an holy' (Mark 6, 20). Herodias waited, then, looking for her opportunity. It came one evening after Herod had given an important banquet for a host of dignitaries (6, 22):

And when the daughter of the said Herodias came in, and danced, and pleased Herod and them that sat with him, the king said unto the damsel, Ask of me whatsoever thou wilt, and I will give it thee. And … she went forth, and said unto her mother, What shall I ask? And she said, The head of John the Baptist.

Beautiful but sinister, this dancing daughter is never named in the Gospel story; the tradition that she was called Salome seems to have originated with the Jewish–Roman historian Josephus. Whatever her name, she is an obvious mythological heir to Delilah, who did for Samson, and a castrating counterbalance to that heroic seductress Judith. She makes a worthy addition to the long line of scriptural femmes fatales.

in the Garden' in Gethsemane. 'Rise', he chided his sleeping apostles (26, 46): 'behold, he is at hand that doth betray me' – even as Judas arrived with 'a great multitude with swords and staves'. Judas now gave his new masters the 'sign' (26, 48) that would see him damned everlastingly in the annals of friendship: 'Whomsoever I shall kiss, that same is he: hold him fast.' It was with a kiss, then, the mark of the dearest love, that he betrayed his friend, condemning him to torture and death.

Too late, the next morning Judas 'repented himself' (27, 3). He took his thirty pieces of silver back to the priests and elders, saying 'I have sinned in that I have betrayed the innocent blood.' Seeing them unmoved, he hurled down the money in the Temple, turned and ran out in an overwhelming fit of grief. And, Matthew calmly notes, 'went and hanged himself':

And the chief priests took the silver pieces, and said, It is not lawful for to put them into the treasury, because it is the price of blood. And they took counsel, and bought with them the potter's field, to bury strangers in. Wherefore that field was called, The field of blood, unto this day. (27, 6)

'I Find No Fault in Him'

Jesus was brought before the Sanhedrin, a priestly court, which mocked and bullied him before finding him guilty of setting himself up as the Son of God. And – in order to couch their condemnation in terms that might mean more

The motive for Judas' treachery is never really explained – it's been attributed to everything from pure monetary greed to a proto-Zionist's disappointment at discovering that what he'd taken as a message of political liberation was really one of personal spiritual salvation.

Whatever his reasons, it seems that Judas went down to see the chief priests (Matthew 26, 14):

What will ye give me, and I will deliver him unto you? And they covenanted with him for thirty pieces of silver. And from that time he sought opportunity to betray him.

That opportunity presented itself when, in the hours after celebrating his Last Supper with his apostles, Jesus was going through his 'Agony

THE TYPE OF THE TRAITOR

JUDAS HAS GONE down in the mythic memory as the embodiment of the traitor: avaricious, opportunistic, selfish – without loyalty or honour. That he took as his sign to the authorities that universal symbol of friendship and affection, a kiss, only underlined the utter coldness of his cynicism.

Jesus' Jewishness, that of every single one of his apostles, and indeed the obvious origins of their religion as a Jewish sect was an endless embarrassment to a Christian Europe that liked to condemn the entire Jewish people as the cruel killers of their saviour. Hence, perhaps, the vilification of one whose very name suggests some special degree of Jewishness, beyond that of his fellow disciples. And, for that matter, his portrayal in art with the flaming red hair and the long, hooked nose that personified the Jew to generations of Europeans – but which, by some Christian miracle, Jesus and the other disciples seem to have been 'spared'.

At the same time, it should be remembered, the Gospel story – and Christian theology – would have been lost without him. Had he not sold out his Lord, where would we all have been? It seems to have been St Augustine who first formulated the idea of the *felix culpa* (the 'happy fault') – the sin that, wicked as it was, would open the way to good. Had not Eve talked Adam into eating the apple, Augustine reasoned, man might have been living in Eden to this day – but the higher paradise of heaven would not have been opened to him. By the same token, some would make the point that Judas' treachery was an essential step in the process by which Christ came to give his life for humankind.

Some early scholars took this view to extreme conclusions, revering Judas for his role in our redemption. Towards the end of the second century, indeed, a *Gospel of Judas* was written. In this account, Judas wasn't just a good apostle but unique in his appreciation of his master's real message, a high-flown spiritualism that left the material world (and the sphere of human love and good works) behind.

Right: Rat-faced, red-haired, stunted ... Judas is the traitor at the table. Joos van Cleve painted this Last Supper in the 1530s. It's to be seen at the Church of Santa Maria della Pace, Rome.

to their Roman Governor, Pontius Pilate – of claiming that he was the 'King of the Jews'. In John's version of these events, Pilate questioned Christ, but was satisfied by his insistence that

---

'The Jews, outraged, challenged him on his loyalty to the empire he was supposed to serve'.

'My kingdom is not of this world' (18, 36): 'I find no fault in him at all' the Governor concluded (18, 38). The Jews, outraged, challenged him on his loyalty to the empire he was supposed to serve: 'If thou let this man go, thou art not Caesar's friend' (19, 12).

Pontius Pilate's washing of his hands (Matthew 27, 24) – to represent that Jesus' fate was no longer to be his problem, nor his responsibility – made him the type of the morally spineless functionary, an early example of that 'banality of evil' Hannah Arendt was to find in the Nazi Obersturmbannführer Adolf Eichmann. Not, however, before centuries of Christian bigots had justified their persecution of the Jews by the verse that follows (27, 25): 'His blood be on us, and on our children.'

Death and Darkness
In the meantime, the blood was all on Christ himself, from his scourging (traditionally at a pillar – although Gospel accounts don't mention this); from his mock crowning with a ring of thorns (Matthew 27, 9); from his nailing to the cross; and to the piercing of his side (John

Left: *Ecce homo!* 'Behold the Man!': Pontius Pilate presents Jesus to the Jewish people in this painting by Antonio Ciseri (1871). Christ appears as a bleakly comic king, his bare back scourged; his head bleeding from a crown of thorns.

STATIONS OF THE CROSS

CATHOLIC TRADITION HAS taken 14 moments from the story of Christ's Passion and Death to make a series of scenes for prayerful contemplation. Most churches have images or carvings of these moments arranged about their interiors: pious Catholics proceed from one to another, praying at each as they make their way through what are called the 'Stations of the Cross'.

1. Jesus is condemned to death.
2. Jesus carries the cross.
3. Jesus falls for the first time.
4. Jesus meets his mother Mary by the roadside.
5. A bystander, Simon of Cyrene, is recruited by the Romans to help Jesus to carry his cross. He seems to have had no choice, but has still come to symbolize the kindness of strangers.
6. Veronica, standing by the roadside and moved with pity for the pain the condemned man is suffering, gives him her veil so that he can wipe his face. He gives it back, and it is imprinted with his face.
7. Jesus falls for the second time.
8. Jesus turns to speak to the weeping women of Jerusalem, who have been following. He tells them (Luke 23, 27) not to weep for him but for themselves and for their children.
9. Jesus falls for the third time.
10. Jesus is stripped of his garments.
11. Jesus is nailed to the cross.
12. Jesus dies on the cross.
13. The 'Deposition'. Jesus, dead, is taken down from the cross.
14. Jesus is laid in the tomb.

Above: Carrying his cross with the help of Simon of Cyrene, Jesus falls amidst his Via Dolorosa; whilst St Veronica prepares her veil to wipe his face. The medieval imagery gets a modern makeover in this stunning stained-glass window.

Not all these scenes have any scriptural basis: the three falls, for example, owe more to medieval symbolism than to anything in the Gospels. As for the St Veronica story, this too is the creation of later Christian tradition – used, perhaps, as a justification for the trade in relics.

19, 31). As for the darkness in this story, that descended literally in the moment of his death:

there was a darkness over all the earth … the sun was darkened, and the veil of the temple was rent in the midst (Luke 23, 24).

An eclipse, an earthquake? Very likely both – fitting mood-music for a deity's death, even if he was (says the scripture) to rise again three days later.

From Pentecost to Persecution

In the days that followed, Christ's disciples were first stunned, then sombre and then sorely afraid. The discovery that their Saviour was once more living was, to begin with, more of a shock than a reassurance. The comfort he brought them was not to last too long. Forty days after the Resurrection, he took his leave for good, ascending to heaven (Acts 1, 10). Now, it seemed, they were utterly alone.

For ten days they sat together, stunned and all but paralyzed, when (2, 2):

suddenly there came a sound from heaven as of a rushing mighty wind, and it filled all the house where they were sitting. And there appeared unto them cloven tongues like as of fire, and it sat upon each of them. And they were all filled with the Holy Ghost, and began to speak with other tongues, as the Spirit gave them utterance.

Emboldened, the first Christians set out to spread the Word. But the Holy Spirit was to offer them no protection – not in this world, at any rate. Those same religious authorities who had led the attack on Christ himself now sought to suppress his followers. St Stephen was to be the

first to feel their wrath. A deacon of the Church, Stephen was hauled up before the Sanhedrin. Like his Lord before him, he made clear that his ambitions were not worldly. He was forthright, though, in his denunciation of their hypocrisy:

Below: 'And there appeared unto them cloven tongues like as of fire …' Pentecost, and the Holy Ghost descends on Christ's disciples where they have been hiding, demoralized and desperate, inspiring them with the courage of his Word.

'They were cut to the heart, and they gnashed on him with their teeth' (7, 54):

Then they cried out with a loud voice, and stopped their ears, and ran upon him with one accord, And cast him out of the city, and stoned him.

From Saul to Paul

Stephen's death was doubly historic, for Christianity's first martyrdom also marked the debut in the scriptural narrative of St Paul. For the moment he was little more than a bystander, although a staunchly anti-Christian one: Stephen's killers 'laid down their clothes at a young man's feet, whose name was Saul' (7, 58).

Though he had a Roman name – Paulus, or Paul – as well, thanks to his father's citizenship, the future disciple appears to have identified more strongly with his Jewish heritage. He was certainly 'consenting unto' St Stephen's execution (8, 1). In fact, the experience galvanized him into action in defence of the faith in which he had been raised: he resolved to dedicate himself to Christianity's eradication, 'breathing out threatenings and slaughter against the disciples of the Lord' (9, 1). It was in pursuit of this objective that, famously, on the road to Damascus, he was felled by a dazzling

Below: Christianity lays its first martyr to rest in the person of St Stephen, stoned to death around the year 36AD. The future St Paul, ironically, was among those present at the execution: he looked after the cloaks of those who were hurling stones.

light from heaven, 'and heard a voice saying unto him, Saul, Saul, why persecutest me?' The speaker then identified himself as Christ.

Above: Close to where the scene it depicts must have taken place, a door of St Peter's Basilica in Rome shows the death of St Peter, the first pope, himself. Peter is said to have been crucified upside down, at his own request.

> 'The only apostle whose martyrdom does find 'official' confirmation in the New Testament is James'.

The rest of St Paul's story is much sweetness and light, despite occasional harassment by the Jewish and Roman authorities. Tradition has it that he was ultimately to die a martyr. In deference to his Roman citizenship, he was beheaded, being spared the grislier and more demeaning end of crucifixion that Christ himself had faced. There's no scriptural basis for this story, though. Neither is there any for the tradition of St Peter's death on a cross – upside-down, it's said, at his own request. Far from finding the idea of crucifixion undignified, the first pope apparently saw himself as unworthy of dying the same death as his Lord and Saviour, so personally asked that the manner of his execution should be changed. The only apostle whose martyrdom does find 'official' confirmation in the New Testament is James, the Brother of John, whom Herod the Great's grandson (Herod Agrippa) executed 'with the sword' (Acts 12, 2).

VIII

REVELATION

'The time is at hand…' warns the Book of Revelation. God will ultimately save his human creation, but before that the battle between good and evil will engulf the world.

◆

'The sun became black … the moon became as blood'.

REVELATION 6, 12.

'I am Alpha and Omega, the beginning and the ending, saith the Lord, which is, and which was, and which is to come, the Almighty' (Revelation 1, 7). Having taken us through the alphabet from the first letter to the last; across a highly-coloured history of humankind from first Creation and Fall to final Redemption, the Bible glances to the future with a disturbing drama of the end times. The

Opposite: 'Behold, he cometh with clouds; and every eye shall see him …' St John, on the island of Patmos, receives that 'Revelation' which Christians have found so memorable – if also so disturbing – down so many generations.

'Revelation of Jesus Christ', we're told, was given by God himself to St John the Divine 'to shew unto his servants things which must shortly come to pass' (Revelation 1, 1). 'Blessed is he that readeth', the text goes on – although the experience doesn't necessarily feel too much of a blessing, given all the tumults and the terrifying traumas it describes.

For it's in these pages that we find the original 'apocalyptic vision'. The Greek word 'apocalypse' means 'revelation' – which doesn't, of course, necessarily have to be so alarming. Here, however, that revelation takes place against a background of prodigious signs and omens that appear in the heavens, on earth and in the oceans. It's from this that the word 'apocalypse' has acquired its popular associations – its suggestion of general upheaval, of volcanoes, earthquakes, thunder and lightning and fiery rain.

For All to See

'Behold,' says the Book of Revelation (1, 7): 'he cometh with clouds; and every eye shall see him, and they also which pierced him: and all kindreds of the earth shall wail because of him.' There is much that is mystic in this concluding book of the Bible, but here, at least – as represented in the phrase 'every eye shall see him' – the revelation could hardly be more literal, more prosaic. Christ our Saviour, it says, will be physically revealed – displayed on high where everyone can see him. There's more to it than this, of course, but even so, in perhaps its most important sense the book's meaning is clear enough. Christ's message will prevail, it promises; his majesty – and the scale of the

Below: 'Out of his mouth went a sharp two-edged sword,' Revelation 1, 16. The Evangelist's vision of the 'Son of Man' amid the 'seven candlesticks', his 'feet like unto fine brass', is one of the most extraordinary images of an extraordinary text.

> 'And I gave her space to repent of her fornication; and she repented not'.
>
> REVELATION 2, 21

sacrifice he has made for us – will be made completely evident to all.

Pretty much immediately, though, the narrative takes a sharp turn towards the much more obscure. 'What thou seest,' says a voice 'as of a trumpet' (1, 10):

write in a book, and send it unto the seven churches which are in Asia … And I turned to see the voice that spoke to me.

It's a strange world in which our narrator John can turn to 'see' a 'voice'; but a far stranger one in which he can see a sight like the following (1, 12):

And being turned, I saw seven golden candlesticks; And in the midst of the seven candlesticks one like unto the Son of man, clothed with a garment down to the foot, and girt about the paps with a golden girdle. His head and his ears were white like wool, as white as snow; and his eyes were as a flame of fire; And his feet like unto fine brass, as if they burned in a furnace; and his voice as the sound of many waters. And he had in his right hand seven stars: and out of his mouth went a sharp twoedged sword ...

He was, he said, 'the first and the last' (1, 17); 'he that liveth, and was dead', but now, 'alive for evermore'.

Jezebel Reborn

He was, in other words, the risen Christ, come to take charge of his Church, hence his messages for Christian communities in Asia Minor (modern Turkey). He gave credit where credit was due, finding much to commend in all these congregations. But he criticized laxness where he saw it, saving the worst of his anger for the church in Thyatira (now Akhisar). There, it seems, a local woman had been preaching to the people, pretending to prophetic powers. Christ compared her with the pagan queen we first encountered in 2 Kings 9 (see p. 146, Chapter 5:

Notwithstanding I have a few things against thee, because thou sufferest that woman Jezebel, which calleth herself a prophetess, to teach and to seduce my servants to commit fornication, and to eat things sacrificed unto idols. And I gave her space to repent of her fornication; and she repented not. Behold, I will cast her into a bed, and them that commit adultery with her into great tribulation, except they repent of their deeds... (2, 22)

Above: The Apocalypse according to Albrecht Dürer. So inspired was the German artist by the Book of Revelation that he brought out his own edition in 1478. This design shows the Chosen Ones and the Saints (those carrying palms).

Seven Seals

The door of heaven opened, John saw a voice 'as it were of a trumpet talking with me' (4, 1) said 'Come up hither, and I will shew thee things which must be hereafter.' Saw an assembly of 'four and twenty elders, sitting, clothed in white raiment; and they had on their heads crowns of gold' (4, 4). At the centre of this gathering, around a throne, stood 'four beasts full of eyes before and behind' (4, 6): they resembled a lion,

Above: The first six seals of the book (5, 1) are breached by the Lamb of God and a succession of startling images are unleashed – most strikingly, the 'Four Horsemen of the Apocalyse'.

a calf, a man and a flying eagle respectively, although each had six wings in addition to its multitude of eyes.

All the elders fell prostrate on the floor before the figure upon the throne, in whose hand could be seen 'a book written within and on the backside, sealed with seven seals' (5, 1). But when an angel demanded to know who of those present was worthy to open the book, John 'wept much,' he says, 'because no man was found worthy to open the book, neither to look thereon' (5, 4).

There too, however, was a lamb standing 'as it had been slain' (5, 6) – the Lamb of God, the sacrificed Christ, in other words. It had 'seven horns and seven eyes' (for Asia Minor's seven churches?). As the elders worshipped before the Lamb, they were thronged about by angels, 'and the number of them was ten thousand ties ten thousand, and thousands of thousands' (5, 11).

Four Horsemen

The Lamb it was who now set about opening each of the seven seals in turn. Amid a sound like that of thunder, a white horse was revealed. Upon it sat an archer, to whom a crown was given. 'He went forth conquering, and to conquer' (6, 2). The opening of the second seal uncovered the sight of a red horse, whose rider wielded a sword given him to enable him 'to take peace from the earth' (6, 4). When the third seal was opened, a black horse could be seen:

Right: 'I saw the seven angels which stood before God; and to them were given seven trumpets … There were voices, and thunderings, and lightnings, and an earthquake. And the seven angels which had the seven trumpets prepared themselves to sound' (8, 6).

THE BEAST

BETWEEN ITS LOCUSTS and its lambs, its calves, its frogs and its eagles, the Book of Revelation is striking in its fauna. Among its most memorable species, however, are those referred to only as 'the beast'. The first appears 'ascendeth out of the bottomless pit' in 11, 7. The second (unless it's the same one), makes its appearance at 13, 1:

And I stood upon the sand of the sea, and saw a beast rise up out of the sea, having seven heads and ten horns, and upon his horns ten crowns, and upon his heads the name of blasphemy.

It was, the description continues (13, 2):

like unto a leopard, and his feet were as the feet of a bear, and his mouth as the mouth of a lion.

His allegiance with Satan was all too clear, however: 'the dragon gave him his power, and his seat, and great authority.'

'Another beast' is seen 'coming up out of the earth' at 13, 11. This one, however:

doeth great wonders, so that he maketh fire come down from heaven on the earth in the sight of men.

It had 'two horns like a lamb', we're told – and we're reminded of the meek and gentle

appearance of the Lamb of God. But since it 'spake as a dragon', giving Satan's message, there's no mistaking the reality: this monster was the devil in sheep's clothing. Since his role, we're told, is to cause earth's inhabitants to 'worship the first beast' (13, 12), this second creature is seen by scholars as emblematic of false prophecy and paganism: it is commonly identified as the 'Antichrist'.

Right: The seven-headed beast of Revelation is depicted with by Lucas Cranach the Elder (c. 1475). Piety apart, the fascination of these phantasmagorical figures for the artists of Reformation Europe isn't difficult to understand.

its rider held up a balance or a scale. The fourth seal was now broken: a 'pale' horse emerged. Mounted upon it was the figure of Death (6, 8):

and Hell followed with him. And power was given unto them over the fourth part of the earth, to kill with sword, and with hunger, and with death, and with the beasts of the earth.

The opening of the fifth seal revealed 'under the altar the souls of them that were slain for the world of God, and for the testimony that they held:

And they cried with a loud voice, saying, How long, O Lord, holy and true, dost thou not judge and avenge our blood on them that dwell on the earth.

The breaching of the sixth seal was the signal for 'a great earthquake' (6, 12):

And the sun became black as sackcloth of hair, and the moon became as blood; And the stars of heaven fell unto the earth, even as a fig tree casteth her untimely figs, when she is shaken of a mighty wind …

And after these things I saw four angels standing on the four corners of the earth, holding the four winds of the earth, that the wind should not blow on the earth, nor on the sea, nor on any tree (7, 1).

Thousands of souls were seen, representing all the different tribes of Israel. They were 'clothed with white robes, and palms in their hands'. Asked how their robes came to be of such a dazzling white, an elder explained (7, 14):

These are they which came out of great tribulation, and have washed their robes, and made them white in the blood of the Lamb.

And when he had opened the seventh seal, there was silence in heaven about the space of half an hour. And I saw the seven angels which stood before God; and to them were given seven trumpets.

Above: 'The fifth angel sounded … And he opened the bottomless pit … And there came out of the smoke locusts upon the earth: and unto them was given power, as the scorpions of the earth have power' (9, 1).

GETTING NERO'S NUMBER

'HERE IS WISDOM', says Revelation (13, 18). 'Let him that hath understanding count the number of the beast.' It is, verse 18 goes on to say, 'Six hundred threescore and six' – that is, 666: a number that haunts fans of horror books and movies to this day.

Was the original 'beast' the Roman Emperor Nero, a cruel persecutor of Christians and (it was widely rumoured) the author of the Great Fire of Rome in 64AD? Many thought so, and further believed that the two were connected. Nero, in this interpretation, having started the terrible conflagration secretly in order to clear some ground he had designs on for an extension to his palace, had been caught off-guard by the backlash. He had therefore sought a scapegoat in Rome's Christian community.

In the special *gematria* number-code the Christians used for secret communications, the figures for Nero came to 666.

THE WHORE OF BABYLON

WHOEVER THE 'WOMAN of the Apocalypse' was, she could hardly have been more different than the 'whore that sitteth upon many waters', to whom we're introduced in Chapter 17 of Revelation. She is one, an angel says, 'with whom the kings of the earth have committed fornication' (17, 2); indeed, her sluttish sins have been a 'wine', intoxicating the people of the earth with sin. 'I saw', says John (17, 3):

a woman sit upon a scarlet coloured beast, full of names of blasphemy, having seven heads and ten horns. And the woman was arrayed in purple and scarlet colour, and decked with gold and precious stones and pearls, having a golden cup in her hand full of abominations and filthiness of her fornication.

Lest there should be any doubt over who she was or the scale of her sinfulness, a name was written 'upon her forehead' (17, 5):

MYSTERY, BABYLON THE GREAT, THE MOTHER OF HARLOTS AND ABOMINATIONS OF THE EARTH.

Babylon by this time belonged in the annals of ancient history; its empire was semi-mythical in its status now. Most early scholars assumed that this imperial whore was really Rome, then mounting cruel persecutions against the followers of Christ. Hence the condition of this woman, 'drunken with the blood of the Saints, and with the blood of the martyrs of Jesus' (17, 6): '*that great city, which reigneth over the kings of the earth* (17, 18).

As, one after another, these angels sounded their trumpets, 'there were voices, and thunderings, and lightnings, and an earthquake' (8, 5); there was more 'hail and fire mingled with blood'. 'A great mountain burning with fire was cast into the sea;' we're told (8, 8): 'and the third part of the sea became blood.'

Locusts from the Smoke

The fifth angel sounded, and, says John (9, 1):

I saw a star fall from heaven unto the earth; and to him was given the key of the bottomless pit. And he opened the bottomless pit; and there arose a smoke out of the pit, as the smoke of a great furnace; and the sun and the air were darkened

by reason of the smoke of the pit.

And, he continues (9, 3):

There came out of the smoke locusts upon the earth; and unto them was given power, as the scorpions of the earth have power ... And the shape of the locusts were like unto horses prepared unto battle; and on their heads were as it were crowns like gold, and their faces were as the faces of men.

Horrific hybrids, these locusts had, we're told (9, 8):

hair as the hair of women, and their teeth were as the teeth of lions ... And the sound of their wings was as the sound of chariots of many horses running to battle. And they had tails like unto scorpions.

A War of Good and Evil

More lightning, more earthquakes and more hailstorms followed before (12, 1) 'there appeared a great wonder in heaven':

A woman clothed with the sun, and the moon

Left: 'Michael and his angels fought ... and Satan, which deceiveth the whole world: he was cast out into the earth' (12, 7). The victorious archangel stands over the vanquished Devil in a stained-glass window inspired by Guido Reni's painting (1636).

A GREAT DAY? REALLY?

ONE OF THE most notorious events of the Revelation narrative is Armageddon, the climactic battle of the end-times. We *do* find mention of 'a place called in the Hebrew tongue Armageddon' (that may or may not be that same 'Megiddo' outside which Josiah's forces failed to smite the Egyptians in 2 Chronicles 35). The spirits of devils, 'working miracles' (16, 14):

go forth unto the kings of the earth and of the whole world, to gather them to the battle of that great day of God Almighty.

That, however, is essentially it. No epic confrontations, no troop-tsunamis or heroic last-stands. Nor any explicit suggestion of a second coming of Christ as the Messiah. No details of any kind, indeed. For an event that has come to loom so large in the imagination (and not

Right: 'And he gathered them together in a place called in the Hebrew tongue Armageddon … And there were voices, and thunders, and lightnings; and there was a great earthquake …' (16, 16), but of the 'battle' which unfolded here there's very little detail.

just that of believers) in modern times, there's remarkably little about this battle in the Bible.

under her feet, and upon her head a crown of twelve stars.

Pregnant, and on the brink of giving birth, she cried out in pain and another wonder appeared on high: this time it was 'a great red dragon, having seven heads, and ten horns, and seven crowns upon his heads' (12, 3). His tail, we're told, 'drew the third part of the stars of heaven, and did cast them to the earth (12, 5):

And the dragon stood before the woman which was ready to be delivered, for to devour her child as soon as it was born.

The man-child she bore was whisked away to heaven and to the throne of God (12, 5), while the woman 'fled into the wilderness':

And there was war in heaven: Michael and his angels fought against the dragon; and the dragon fought and his angels, And prevailed not; neither was their place found any more in heaven. And the great dragon was cast out, that old serpent, called the Devil, and Satan, which deceiveth the whole world (12, 9).

Who was this woman? The Virgin Mary, perhaps? That would explain the man-child.

It's been the view of the Catholic Church down many centuries that this is so. But Protestant commentators, for whom Our Lady never had quite the same significance, have tended to see her as allegorically representing 'Mother Church', her 'man-child' its faithful members.

Death and Judgment

In its final chapters, Revelation rushes towards a triumphant climax: the creation of 'a new heaven and a new earth' (21, 1). 'And I John', says our narrator, naming himself in his sheer joy and pride:

saw the holy city, new Jerusalem, coming down from God out of heaven, prepared as a bride adorned for her husband.

Here the blessed will live for ever: 'there shall be no more death, neither sorrow, nor crying, neither shall there be any more pain: for the former things are passed away' (21, 4). But the new scheme is binary by its very nature – the beauty of the new order lies in its symmetry, and this dictates that the saving of the virtuous must be balanced by the damnation of the rest. If 'he that overcometh' is to 'inherit all things' (21, 7), the divine logic of the Lord demands that:

the fearful, and unbelieving, and the abominable, and murderers, and whoremongers, and sorcerers, and idolaters, and all liars, shall have their part in the lake which burneth with fire and brimstone: which is the second death.

Below: The Last Judgment, as described in Revelation 21 and depicted by Fra Angelico in a 'winged' altarpiece of c. 1450. Christ sits throned in majesty, whilst the souls of the saved are separated from the sinners in the scene below.

GOSPEL TRUTH?

The Bible has a 'dark history' all of its own: patched together from a range of sources, its claims to authority were controversial from the start.

◆

'*Whatsoever things were written aforetime were written for our learning.*' ROMANS 15, 4.

I n the beginning was the Word ...' The famous opening of St John's Gospel obviously echoes that of Genesis – as though setting scripture on the same sort of footing as the world. Quite a claim, yet not unjustified: the Word, as encountered in the Bible, has certainly been the foundation of faith for countless generations – for Jews, for Christians and to some extent for Muslims too.

Opposite: Christ holds up the Gospel of St John as though endorsing it in this icon from the Agiou Pavlou Monastery of Mount Athos, Chalkidiki, Greece. Even for believers, questions are to be faced as to how exactly such books should be read.

But, to put it bluntly, is the Good Book as good as its word?

The question is not simply whether the scriptural account is literally 'true': whether there's the same accumulation of evidence for the historicity of Christ as there is for that of, say, George Washington or Winston Churchill. The answer to that question has to be a brief and brutal 'No' – although it's not a question that most Christians would be inclined to ask. As for Old Testament figures such as Cain and Abel, Adam and Eve, Jeremiah, Jonah or Ezekiel, only extreme fundamentalists see their stories as being 'true' in anything like a literal sense. But they are, of course, entitled to that belief.

Beyond the basic facts, there's the more elusive question of how some sort of straightforward 'truth' is to be elicited from so vast (and often contradictory) a text. It's not just that the Bible is susceptible to readings that

erat uerbum. & uerbum erat apud dīn. & deus
erat uerbū. hoc erat in principio apud dīn. Oīa
pīpsū facta sunt. & sine ipso sacrum est nichil.
Quod factū ē. in ipso uita erat. & uita erat lux
homnū. & lux in tenebris lucet. & tenebre eam
non cōprehendert. fuyt homo missus a dō cuyus

lumine. Erat lux uera. que illuminat onnīe ho
mīne uenīente in hunc mundū. In mundo erat et
mundo pīpsū fact ē. & mundus eū non cognouyt.
In propria uenīt. & sui eū non recepert. Quotqt aute
recepert eum. dedit eis potestate filios dī fierihis
q credunt in nomine ej. Qui ñ ex sanguinib. neq:

may be wrong-headed or deliberately perverse ('the devil can cite scripture for his purpose', Shakespeare said). Written texts are by their very nature open to interpretation, and the bigger and more complex they are the more interpretations they make available.

'He Saith True'

'And he that saw it bare record, and his record is true: and he knoweth that he saith true, that ye might believe.' While all the Gospels set forth their narratives as fact, this assertion – in St John's account of Christ's crucifixion (19, 35) – is the nearest we have to a declaration that what is described actually, literally happened and

> 'It's not just that the Bible is susceptible to readings that may be wrong-headed or deliberately perverse'.

has been verified. The Old Testament, however stentorian its tone of authoritativeness may be, doesn't trouble to make this sort of claim.

For what it's worth, few scholars believe that St John did really witness the events he described – or even that there was any single man named 'John'. Still less do they credit the claim that the author of this text was the Apostle John. Rather, they think, this powerful text was

Left: Around a floridly illuminated 'In Principio' (for 'In the Beginning ...') St John's Gospel gets under way in an explosive swirl of ornamentation in this early Latin Vulgate edition. Christ looks on from above while the Evangelist writes.

Right: His right hand raised in blessing, his face severe with rectitude, St John cuts an utterly credible figure in this stained-glass widow from St Gregory's Church, Offchurch, Warwickshire. But might his air of authority be misleading?

the work of a community of Christians, writing towards the end of the first century AD. While the other gospels set out the life and works of Christ then leave it up to their readers to draw the obvious conclusion of Jesus' divinity and the greatness of his Church, John's Gospel starts out with its Christian standpoint fully-formed.

But the other gospels were written only slightly earlier, it seems. Matthew's seems to have been completed some time in the decade between 80 and 90 AD (although its authorship

+ Sˢ IOHANNES +

PROGRESS TOWARDS THE PAST

IT GOES WITHOUT saying that the scripture has been read in different ways at different times. The temptation for us, in an age of self-conscious sophistication, is to see this as a gradual change from literal-minded credulity to a more metaphorical view of mythic narrative and spiritual 'subtext'. This view, apparently so sceptical, is actually an aspect of our own modern 'myth of progress': the idea that the Bible should be read as factually 'true' is a surprisingly new one.

As long ago as medieval times, Catholic scholars saw the Old Testament as a mythic, mystic text whose deeper truths were to be drawn out by exegesis or interpretation. The Catholic way was, in any case, for the clergy to explain Christ's teachings to largely uneducated, even illiterate, congregations. The Church's authority was at stake, its Latin scripture the exclusive property of the hierarchy: attempts to translate it were at times to be savagely suppressed. At the same time, this elitist view encouraged what we might see as a more 'modern' view of the Bible as a text to be interpreted, rather than as a straightforward record of actual events.

A more democratic reformed religion believed that the Bible belonged in the hands of believers: Martin Luther made his own translation between 1522 and 1534. Protestants read avidly: the Bible was their daily spiritual sustenance in a way it never had been previously, even for the most pious. Its stories stocked their minds; its imagery possessed their imagination; biblical characters became the companions of their lives.

The Enlightenment and the advent of modern science made religious belief more problematic, fostering confusion and uncertainty: many rejected religion out of hand. At the same time, though, in encouraging new standards in 'truth', a new sense of what it was to believe in something, these changes may, paradoxically, have produced a more literal-minded approach to the Bible among believers. Certainly, it was in the 1890s, when so many intellectuals were making the agonized journey to scientific atheism, that Christian fundamentalism was born.

Above: Expression stern, Martin Luther faces down his Catholic critics. Standing beside a lectern, he's shown with a finger pointing at the Bible, the basis of his authority – the only basis, he maintained, for any religious authority.

was then anonymous: the attribution 'according to Matthew' dates from the second century AD). Mark's Gospel, by some way the shortest, was written in the 60s. It has taken second place in the traditional running because it was assumed to have been a summary of Matthew's. Actually, in all probability it was the other way round: Matthew's Gospel reworked and expanded Mark's bare-bones account. (The 'extra' material deals with the doctrinal details of Jesus' teachings on the one hand, and ways in which his words and actions fulfilled Old Testament prophecies on the other.) Luke's Gospel, like the Acts of the Apostles (both of which are thought to have been written by the same person), is believed to date from some time around the year 80 AD.

Contested Compositions

If there's a certain amount of controversy over the authorship of the Gospels, this is nothing to the debate that's raged over other, more marginal works. More marginal works which, however, have at one time or another had their pretensions to being part of sacred scripture.

The *apocryphal gospels* are a loose collection of sources that purport to tell the story of Christ on the same sort of basis as the four officially-recognized or 'canonical' gospels – those of Matthew, Mark, Luke and John. Derived from the Greek for 'hidden' or 'secret', the word *apocryphal* implies a dubiousness of status. (The story of George Washington and

Above: With his focus on the humanity of Christ, St Matthew has a winged man – or an angel – as his symbol. Such a figure helps him write his Gospel in this painting from Venice's Church of Santa Maria della Salute (by Antonio Triva da Reggio, 1626).

the cherry tree has generally been deemed 'apocryphal', for example.) Some apocrypha in fact follow the established accounts quite closely – they remain outside the canon mainly because their independent composition can't be established. Others depart more radically from the mainstream sources, whether

SYNOPTIC OPTIONS

MATTHEW'S, MARK'S AND Luke's accounts are known collectively as the 'synoptic gospels', leaving the Gospel of St John as the odd one out. The word 'synoptic' is Greek in origin: 'syn' means together (as in 'synthesis' or 'synergy') while 'optic' means 'sight' or 'view' (as in 'optician'). Just as the 'synopsis' of a film or novel might give an at-a-glance overview of a big and complex narrative, the synoptic gospels present Christ's life concisely and straightforwardly. But they're also 'synoptic' in the sense that they share a perspective on their subject: all present much the same material in substantially the same way. John's Gospel, while resembling the others in having at its heart a narration of the life, actions and teachings of Jesus Christ, seems to have drawn on different sources.

venturing into the sort of mystic depths the canonical gospels skirt around, or attempting to fill in the 'gaps' in the official version. Hence the attempts of many early writers to describe the childhood years of Jesus, before he embarked on his ministry.

The New Testament apocrypha include certain subsets, such as the *pseudepigrapha* – so called because they were falsely attributed by their writers to earlier (and generally more famous) authors. The Gospel of Barnabas was one example – as was that of Judas: both date from the end of the second century AD or even later. Then there are the *antilegomena* – works whose authenticity, although accepted by some, is in dispute. For the most part these are excluded from the canon. Some remain, however – the most striking by some distance being the Book of Revelation, whose canonicity was questioned by many in the early Church (and by later reformers like Martin Luther and John Calvin).

The Old Testament also has those

Left: St Mark in stained glass by a German master craftsman of the nineteenth century. He stands amidst the splendour of his church. The sword betokens courage (his traditional symbol was the lion); the scroll the Gospel he gave us.

Right: From St Peter's Church on the Channel Island of Sark, UK, comes this image of St Luke in a stained-glass window, a quill in his right hand as he writes his Gospel. Luke also wrote the Acts of the Apostles.

deuterocanonical books that make it into the Catholic canon but not the Jewish – or, in most cases, the Protestant. Along with the Book of Judith, these include certain additions to the Books of Daniel and Esther as well as the Books of Tobit, Wisdom and 1 and 2 Maccabees.

The Dead Sea Scrolls

It was in 1946 that a Bedouin shepherd stumbled on a small cache of ancient texts, concealed in jars in a cave at Qumran in what is now the Palestinian Territory of the West Bank. Seven scrolls were found at first – the best part of a thousand were to follow as researchers investigated what turned out to be a network of caves, once apparently occupied by a community of Essenes. Members of a breakaway sect, the Essenes practised a particularly ascetic form of Judaism and lived in isolated communities in desert regions – like that around the shores of the Dead Sea.

Written on parchment and papyrus in a range of ancient languages, from Hebrew and

AN UNCHRISTIAN CHRIST

ONE OF A series of apocryphal texts that tackle the 'missing' years of Jesus' early upbringing, the *Infancy Gospel of Thomas* paints its subject in the most unpleasant colours. Its utterly implausible attribution to the Apostle Thomas qualifies it as pseudepigraphal: the dates wouldn't fit his authorship, even if the doctrine did.

The boy Jesus, 'Thomas' asks us to believe, puts a curse on a boy who crosses him as a one-year old: his unfortunate enemy immediately falls down dead. Another boy, accidentally bumping into our future Saviour, is also cursed and pays for his clumsiness with his life. When neighbours in Nazareth complain about Jesus' vengeful acts they are immediately blinded by his miraculous powers.

Aramaic to Greek, these scrolls dated back as far as the fifth century BCE – and to as recently as the fourth century CE. While many were simply copies of known biblical texts, others may have been political and spiritual writings by the Essenes and other groups.

Yet another set of texts seem to have been scriptural writings – although not books accepted as canonical by Jewish (or Christian) Bible scholars. These include the Books of Enoch and Jubilees and several psalms.

Lost in Translations

The Old Testament presents itself, in the first instance, as a history of the Jews. Not surprisingly, then, it was written in Hebrew. The New Testament is a different case: while to begin with, under Peter's leadership, Christianity remained closely associated with

Above: A fragment of one of the Dead Sea Scrolls, a veritable treasure-trove of scriptural and other writings (almost a thousand documents in all) stumbled upon by a Bedouin herdsman at Qumran, in the West Bank, in 1946.

Right: A 'codex' is handwritten, but bound up like a modern printed book. Though incomplete when, in 1845, it was found at the Orthodox St Catherine's Monastery, in Sinai, the 'Codex Sinaiticus' gives the bulk of the Bible in fourth-century Greek.

its Jewish origins, St Paul pushed for it to engage with – and to proselytize in – a wider world.

The eastern Mediterranean and Middle East had since the time of Alexander the Great been under the sway of a Hellenic (or Greek) culture. This had remained true to a great extent even under Roman rule. When not directed to congregations in Greece itself (the Corinthians;

the Thessalonians; the Philippians ...), Paul's Epistles are often directed to Greek-speaking groups in Asia Minor (the Ephesians; the Galatians ...). Even the Epistle to the Romans was written in Greek rather than Latin.

It was natural, then, for the New Testament as a whole to have been written in Greek as well – even when its authors were Judaean Jews. (The Old Testament too had for quite some time been readily accessible in Greek: the so-called Septuagint – named in Latin for the 70 scholars supposedly engaged in its translation – had been completed by the end of the second century BCE.)

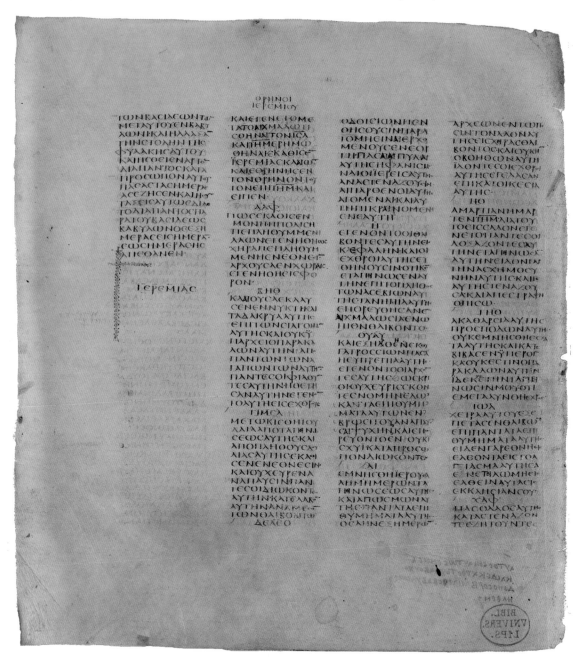

THE MACCABEES

THE FIRST AND Second Books of the Maccabees describe the heroic resistance of the Jews to Hellenic (Greek) domination in the second century BCE. When Alexander the Great swept through the region in the fourth century BCE, Judaea went barely unnoticed among his conquests. History's greatest military commander was to take possession of the Egypt of the Pharaohs as well as the vastness of Persia's empire in the east. When he died in 323 BCE, his generals carved up his realms: Seleucus Nicator, having drawn an eastern section centring on Persia, started pushing westward at his rivals' expense. The 'Seleucid' dynasty he founded was to hold sway here for generations.

By the second century BCE, however, Seleucid rule was starting to look shaky. Local rebellions were flaring up across the east. Judaea seemed peaceful enough until King Antiochus IV attempted to bring greater stability to his empire with an aggressive programme of Hellenization, which involved the stamping out of local cultures and religious practices.

This crackdown caused profound resentment among many peoples of the Empire. In 166 BCE, young Jewish men rose up under the leadership of Judas Maccabaeus. Guerrilla fighters for religious freedom, they inflicted major reversals on Antiochus' forces. In 165 BCE, they took back control of Jerusalem with its Temple (an event commemorated to this day in the festival of Hannukah), although

finally they were to be cruelly put down.

The First and Second Books of the Maccabees describe these events – albeit with a positive spin, their narrative stopping short before the suppression of the rising. There are also a Third and Fourth book, though, anachronistically, the former describes a much earlier revolt against Seleucid rule, while the latter – more spiritual in its focus – takes the martyrdom of the Maccabees as a starting point for a much more spiritual exploration of what it is to live and die in faith.

Right: 'And the temple of Dagon, with them that were fled into it, he burned with fire' (1 Maccabees 10, 84). The Maccabean rebels saw their fight as a holy war – as much against Middle Eastern paganism as against the occupying Greeks.

Right: 'The jewel of the clergy has become the toy of the laity,' conservative critics complained, when Wycliffe's English Bible first appeared in 1382. In this illuminated version, the new text is prestigiously presented itself – its real threat lay in its empowering of the poor.

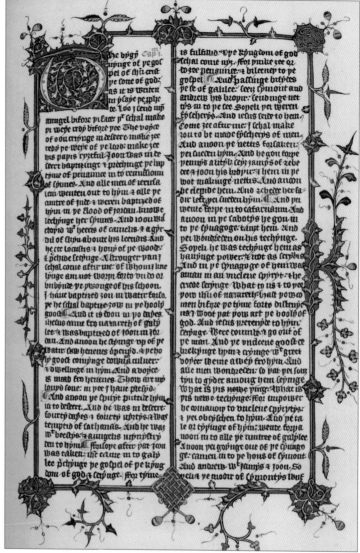

Vulgate vs Vernacular

Rome, however, was the centre of the world – hence its importance to Saints Peter and Paul, both of whom were to die there. It seemed only natural for the papacy to be established in the world's metropolis – and to preside over a Latin-speaking Church. By 200 AD, Hebrew texts were being translated for what was later to be known as the *Vetus Latina* ('Old Latin'), to distinguish it from the fourth-century Vulgate, translated by St Jerome from 382 AD.

The Church's hostility to the translation of the Bible can be overstated. Complete or partial vernacular versions of the scripture appeared in several languages in the Middle Ages, with the blessing of the Church. These would not have been widely available to ordinary people, though: the Church's crackdowns on translations (as with Wycliffe's Bible in fourteenth-century England) came when senior clergy feared that they formed part of wider democratizing movements.

The real hardening of attitudes came with the Counter-Reformation, when the Catholic Church sought to fight Protestant passion with a reforming fire of its own. In reaction to the Protestants' translation-drive, Rome relaunched the Latin liturgy and scripture in all their ancient mystique: what they lacked in clarity they made up for in authority and force. Accordingly it was at the Council of Trent (1545–63) – over 1000 years after its first publication – that the Vulgate was formally adopted as the official Bible of the Church.

Exit England

By that time it was too late – for English Catholics, at least. Henry VIII had broken with

THE SIBYLLINE ORACLES

THE ORIGINAL SIBYLS lived in ancient Greece: old wise women, they interpreted the oracles that came issuing from the earth at shrines like Delphi. One Sibyl appears in Virgil's Roman epic, the *Aeneid*: she guides the hero Aeneas to an entrance into the Underworld when he ventures down among the dead to meet his departed father Anchises.

Like the shamans of later tribal religions, the Sibyls became possessed by the deities who spoke through them: they prophesied in a trance, speaking in a stream of riddles. Hence the title, *The Sibylline Oracles*, bestowed on a later work, dating from about the second century AD onwards, and written in Greek, although comprising a strange stew of ancient pagan, classical Christian and Jewish lore. All are obscure, to a greater or lesser degree, although some appear to offer commentary on passages from the Bible – including some resembling verses from the Book of Revelation.

the Roman Church. The annulment of his marriage to Catherine of Aragon refused, he had quarrelled with the Catholic hierarchy and, in 1534, set himself up as head of the Church of England. It was, to begin with at least, a change only in management: in its theological content, church teaching stayed the same. Brief as it was, though, the reign of Henry's sickly young son was long enough to allow a major shift towards Protestantism: Edward VI was a serious thinker and a fearless reformer.

His successor, Mary I, was ruthless in her attempts to turn the clock back to Catholicism, but 'Bloody Mary' faced a fight in a country that had left its former faith behind. And her failure to produce an heir opened the door to Elizabeth, her half-sister. The daughter of Anne Boleyn, for whom Mary's mother had been put aside, she owed her existence to her father's break with Rome.

Left: The Tiburtine Sibyl tells Augustus of the imminent coming of Christ. A sceptical-looking Emperor gazes skyward. Some early Christians were as quick as their enemies to confuse Christ's message and see their Saviour as a ruler for this earth.

'The reign of Henry's sickly young son was long enough to allow a major shift towards Protestantism'.

Elizabeth too died childless, making way for James VI of Scotland to reign as James I. Although his mother, Mary Queen of Scots, had been a committed Catholic, she had been compelled to accept that her son be brought up a Protestant.

The King James Bible

Despite the suspicions of some in England, James was staunchly Protestant in his views. He listened to complaints from puritans that the Anglican Bibles of Henry and Elizabeth's reigns had continued to be tainted with Romish tones. In 1604, King James called together representatives of the country's clergy for a conference at Hampton Court where it was agreed that a new translation would be taken in hand.

All 47 scholars who worked on the King James Bible were members of the Church of England: they worked collaboratively, in little committees in which both 'high' (more Catholic) and 'low' (more Protestant-puritanical) traditions were represented. The Catholic Vulgate was kept on hand for help with particularly knotty cruces, but the translators worked, where possible, directly from ancient Hebrew, Greek and Aramaic sources.

The English text they came up with has been acclaimed in the centuries since as one of the greatest works of literature in the language – a language changed irrevocably by this Bible, its

Below: 'Heed not the alien minister,/Nor his creed without reason or faith:/For the foundation stone of his temple/Is the bollocks of Henry VIII.' A harsh assessment from the Irish poet. The English king sends Catherine of Aragon packing.

Right: An impressive frontispiece for an important tome. The King James Bible was a religious, a political and a patriotic project, commissioned by the King to embody and articulate an English Christianity for an established English Church.

vocabulary and its rhythms. While this wasn't the translators' primary intention, they certainly *did* intend the text to have a special dignity, and so it's proved. Time and again, it turns out, they favoured slight archaisms against contemporary idioms, to achieve an augustness of tone; they selected more sonorous words where lighter, more prosaic ones were available. The same went for syntax, more elaborate Latinate forms being chosen where more straightforward, English-sounding phrases would have done the job. All in all, they looked for forms of words that would do full justice to the 'Word'. Few would dispute that they found them.

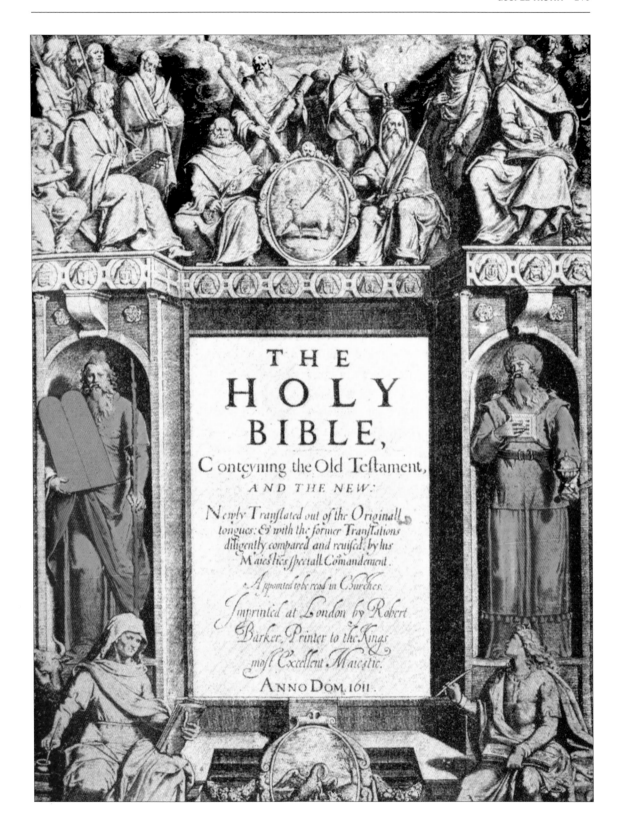

THE
HOLY
BIBLE,

Conteyning the Old Testament,
AND THE NEW:

Newly Translated out of the Originall
tongues: & with the former Translations
diligently compared and revised, by his
Maiesties speciall Comandement.

Appointed to be read in Churches.

Imprinted at London by Robert
Barker, Printer to the Kings
most Excellent Maiestie.

ANNO DOM. 1611.

INDEX

PICTURE CREDITS

Alamy: 2 (Peter Horree), 12 (Classic Image), 19 (Peter Horree), 20 (Fine Art), 24 (Peter Barritt), 26 (Florilegius), 29 (Peter Horree), 36 (Ivy Close Images), 51 (Robert Harding), 52 (Print Collector), 57 (Superstock), 73 (Niday Picture Library), 118 (Active Museum), 125 (Billwissedition), 135 (AGE Fotostock), 149 (Peter Horree), 158 (Image Broker), 161 (Artepics), 166/167 (Niday Picture Library), 174/175 (Chris Hellier), 179 (Robert Harding), 183 (Active Museum), 188 (Joris van Ostaeyen), 190 (Print Collector), 191 (Robert Harding), 193 (Interfoto), 196 (Billwissedition), 198 (Interfoto), 200 (ASP Religion), 205 (Image Broker), 207 (Colin Underhill), 211 (David Askham)

Alamy/Art Archive: 10, 18, 45, 50, 55 top, 58, 84, 136/137, 156, 178, 180, 185, 197, 199, 210

Alamy/BibleLandPictures: 70, 85, 150-155 all, 213

Alamy/Heritage Image Partnership: 1, 62, 69, 87, 122, 138, 147 bottom, 181, 203

Alamy/Lebrecht: 8, 39, 46, 60, 61, 72, 76, 77, 78, 82, 89, 108, 113, 133, 139, 143, 144, 147 top, 159, 168, 176, 215, 216, 218

Alamy/North Wind Picture Archive: 6, 13, 15, 42, 56, 90, 104, 164

Alamy/Prisma Archivo: 11, 63, 141, 148, 192, 214

Alamy/World History Archive: 43, 59, 66/67, 83, 186/187, 195

Corbis: 30 (Geoffrey Clements), 95 (Burstein Collection), 124 (Historical Picture Archive), 127 (Art Archive), 204 (Julian Kumar/Godong), 206 (Stapleton Collection)

Depositphotos/Nicku: 162, 163, 171, 172, 202

Depositphotos/Ruskpp: 25, 38, 121, 131

Dreamstime: 109 (Nicku), 115-117 all (Nicku), 120 (Josef Sedmak), 130 (Josef Sedmak), 189 (Peeterson), 209 (Josef Sedmak)

Mary Evans Picture Library: 16, 21, 22, 31, 32, 33, 40, 41, 55 bottom, 64, 65, 68, 75, 79, 86, 101, 112, 114, 126, 128, 134 (Douglas McCarthy), 140, 145, 157 (Reuben Luke), 165, 169, 177, 184, 194 (Paul Maeyaert/Iberfoto)

Werner Forman Archive: 23 (Louvre Museum), 48

Fotolia: 37 (James Steidl), 88 (Nicku), 111 (Erica Guilane-Nachez), 212 (Byjeng)

Getty Images: 14 (De Agostini), 17 (De Agostini), 44 (Bridgeman Art Library), 47 (Superstock), 49 (National Geographic), 71 (Bridgeman Art Library), 80 (Universal Images), 96 (Bridgeman Art Library), 99 (Bridgeman Art Library), 102, 123 (Superstock)

Getty/Hulton: 7, 74, 81, 91, 92/93, 94, 100, 105, 106, 110, 129, 132, 219

Library of Congress: 34/35, 208

TopFoto: 103 (British Library)